Colombo to Colombo
A Cycling Adventure Around Sri Lanka

Daniel Doughty

DSD UK Publishing

Daniel Doughty

ALSO BY DANIEL DOUGHTY

Tokyo to Tokyo : A Cycling Adventure Around Japan

Colombo to Colombo : A Cycling Adventure Around Sri Lanka

First Published in Great Britain - 2024

Copyright© Daniel Doughty, 2024

Published by DSD UK Publishing
www.travelbloke.co.uk
dsd_uk@yahoo.co.uk

Cover by Gillian Hibbs
Map by Daniel Doughty

All rights reserved.

No part of this book may be reproduced by any means, nor transmitted, nor translated into a machine language, without the written permission of the publisher.

Daniel Doughty has asserted his right to be identified as the author of this work in accordance with sections 77 and 78 of the Copyright, Designs and Patents Act 1988.

Condition of Sale:
This book is sold subject to the condition that it shall not, by way of trade or otherwise, be lent, re-sold, hired out or otherwise circulated in any form binding or cover, other than that in which it is published and without a similar condition including this condition being imposed on the subsequent purchaser.

ISBN: 978-0-9955534-2-2

In loving memory of
Nanny Else & Grandad Len

Longing for the Road

It is on the road that I feel most at home. Far, far away from the stresses and the woes of an accountable existence; that with every year of passing degrades and blemishes. A place where the sweat becomes my fee and the dirt my earnings. Just over the horizon, there is always a place with new faces, cultures, delicacies and stories that yearn for discovery. With more questions than answers, there is a near innocence to such curious and often guileless gallivanting. Out there and beyond, it draws me in, it always has done, without conviction or judgement. To pertain to such a solipsism of self for just the sheerest moment in time, that is to live. To rub shoulders with the unknown mysteries of the world, before retreating back to the inevitable mundane, or the so often referred to daily grind. Out there on the road, through fields and valleys and out to the windswept coasts there exists a freedom like no other; a freedom reliably called 'luck,' where the balance of mind can be truly restored. The road therefore is my antidote, and like that of a migrating hirundine there is a boundless conviction as to where home truly lay. Regardless, I will forever be drawn to the road. I know no other way.

*

In 2014, when I was the first self-proclaimed English dipshit to cycle to all 47 of Japan's prefectures, it took the sinisterly charmless taste of dog shit to spark an intervention. This time around however, dog shit I am pleased to confirm played no part in the tale. Just an all round general longing to return to what I truly loved. The bug was back and it sought its fix. A bug that deep down I knew would never truly leave me, that much I'll always know.

The years had flashed past since Japan, a country where having spent some considerable time I had acquired some semblance of place. I even spoke a little of the language; albeit quite badly I should add. But nonetheless, with its idyllic roads, charming locals, delicious cuisine, inspiring countryside and 7-Elevens strategically placed around every given corner, Japan was markedly a land of unabashed convenience - and rightly so too. That's not to say that Japan didn't go without a chaotic array of hiccups, for if it didn't I would have never have been able to write the trashy force *majeure* that was 'Tokyo to Tokyo: A Cycling Adventure Around Japan,' available now from all good retailers and probably some shitty ones too. But, that was then, and the dawn of a new challenge beckoned and it beckoned hard. Where and how was still all to play for, but it would generally have to be a place that I can sweat my tits off as opposed to freeze them off, that was a bonafide dealbreaker. I rummaged around in my spacious head for some ideas with largely fruitless abandon: *Clay Pigeon Shooting Across the Americas with Richard and Judy, Swimming the Atlantic on Smack, Looking for Space Junk in the Congo, Around the World with 23 Pumpkins or Tandem Cycling Europe with Bob Nudd.* Mere concepts really that generally lacked any sort of punitive initiative. The only thing that definitely did feel completely right and wholesomely purposeful was indeed the bicycling part. Something that if you've made it past the front cover you've probably already more than clocked anyway. In fact, you already 100% know where I'm going and what it is I'm doing, such is the nature of the complete and utter spoiler of this books very title; 'Keep it simple, keep it functional,' said my editor; to which I bent the knee too with superfluous glee. But still, to know why such a thing should come about is perhaps just as important, its not, but it feels like it should be. Apologies, I digress.

Tour cycling though, I am truly hooked on that shit. There aren't too many better ways in which to explore a destination. Not too slow, not too fast. An elegant pace in a way. To watch the world unfurl in slow motion is to watch the world tick. Cliche perhaps, but true no less. So yes, it simply had to be a bicycle ride.

My journey need not be endlessly long, for I had neither the time nor the funds. I did however feel the comparative need to stray away from orderliness and structure. I needed roads that gave false negatives as a first impression. Roads that titillated and bamboozled. Roads that ideally, were just plain fucked. So therefore the experience that I so craved with pastures new and slightly fucked, needed in itself to be perceivably raw. If

I could nearly break myself mentally and physically whilst reaping the buoyant and priceless memories that are so often gifted through travel, then my sick little vice would surely be sought.

Deciding where to embark upon however isn't quite as haphazard as just closing one's eyes and throwing a dart at a map. With that method there's a 75% chance you'll end up needing to be either a very strong swimmer, or at least having in your possession a set of gills; preferably both. Alas, I had no such attributes, I am merely a simple landlubberly myrmidon. The decision in the end though was far less complex than I could have ever of imagined and one that hit me when I least expected it. I'll set the scene. It was a cold and wet wintery Sunday afternoon in the Fens of Cambridgeshire. A bleak place at the best of times, but one of several places on this revolving sphere of ours that I'd come to call home. Unfortunately, it was still far too early in the day for Babestation and therefore I was destined to channel surf through a rampant array of televised dross; visualised shit in the purest sense if you please. With each channel I passed through my commentary went a little something like this: 'Shit, shit, more shit, absolute shit, that guy's a dick, shit, steaming shit, shit, she's a dick too, shit, shit!! Oh, it's Rick Stein, nice!' Well, what can I say? I'm a sucker for a good cooking show! But on this very occasion little did Rick or myself know that Rick's show would garnish me with just the kind of zesty inflatus that I so desired.

Rick strolled a distant beach in his vivid pink shirt, sweating his tits off upon sand as soft as butter. The azure waters behind him idly caressed the shoreline and made for a romantic notion. He dined in local curry houses, ate the street food and experienced the freshest of fish straight out of the ocean and onto his plate. Inspired by his travels, Rick situated in his home kitchen lobbed a bunch of vibrant and fiery looking ingredients into his fat wok as he set about cooking up a mean and mouth watering cashew curry. I dribbled down my chin slightly. *Hmm...Sri Lanka*, my curiosity had been piqued.

It was a country that despite all of my travel exploits over the decades I still hadn't investigated. I suddenly began to envisage mystery dirt tracks that trailed off into wild jungle, rough-hewn mountain paths enveloped in mist and euphoric coastal roads that meandered for endless miles. Not to mention the endless curry jaunts, cold beer, fine tea, dreamy sunsets and exotic wildlife that could either crush you to death or eat you for dinner, or of course very much both. Yes, Sri Lanka! This must surely be the place, I was certain of it. A virgin land to my nearly completely near knackered passport and one that would assuredly quench my thirst for something just that little bit more inconvenient.

Even though my stage was set for 2018, in 2019 Sri Lanka was voted top place to travel by the Lonely Planet. A stat I wouldn't have known at the time but one still worth mentioning as a segway to a slightly more gruelling stat. In 2017, Sri Lanka was only second to Puerto Rico on the Global Climate Risk index as one of the most natural disaster prone countries on the planet. Unfortunately, the island with its double monsoon season very rarely leaves this complete harbinger of a 'Top 10,' being bedevilled on an annual basis by mass flooding and landslides. And then, there was the Boxing Day 2004 tragedy, whereby the island was shaken by one of the world's most devastating tsunamis in living memory - with Sri Lanka being only second to that of Indonesia for the greatest loss of life. Peel a little more beneath the layers and this tropical paradise denotes an even darker tone. For nearly 30 long years bullets and mortar divided the country in an horrific civil war where countless lives were lost - most of them innocent civilians. These are the kinds of scars that cut deep within a nation, the kind of scars that would still bleed for many years to come and probably never truly heal.

As with cycling the haunting tsunami stricken Tōhoku coastline of Japan in 2014, where the dread for a time felt perpetual, I knew that this challenge at times would add a mental element to factor in with the physical one. A mental challenge that in my opinion far outweighed the physical aspect, but one all the same that would educate and give perspective.

My formula for approaching the task in hand wouldn't change that much to my previous partaking. It would of course consist of being a half-baked plan, as to plan too far ahead when travelling is dutifully imbecilic. Because plans, like even the best of them have a tendency to change. It's just something that they always seem to do. In Japan though, I cycled all 47 of the country's prefectures, it seemed only apt to commit to something similar. Sri Lanka however, doesn't have prefectures, it has districts - 25 of them all in all. And so, in a roundabout fashion I planned to cycle through all of them. I'd cover the necessary ground, get myself off the beaten track, learn through trial and error, maybe even get myself a little lost and experience more than I'd intended. I'd probably also get pissed up a few times too; in fact that is probably the one thing that before setting off I could well confirm as something that will most definitely be happening…at some point.

But Dan mate, what does this all prove? I sense you reel. Really I do. Well, by and large just as before, a vast amount of sweet fuck all. It just felt right… at the time.

Daniel Doughty

CONTENTS

Prologue, 6
1. Colombo, 16
2. Kandy, 31
3. Kurunegala, 38
4. Gampaha, 42
5. Puttalam, 48
6. Mannar, 76
7. Vavuniya, 89
8. Mullaitivu, 93*, 120**
9. Kilinochchi, 100
10. Jaffna, 107
11. Trincomalee, 129
12. Anuradhapura, 136
13. Matale, 147
14. Polonnaruwa, 158
15. Batticaloa, 165
16. Ampara, 174
17. Monaragala, 183
18 Badulla, 185
19. Nuwara Eliya, 206
20. Kegalle, 217
21. Ratnapura, 221
22. Matara, 231*, 237 **
23. Hambantota, 233
24. Galle, 249
25. Kalutara, 267
Colombo : A Return, 270

1. Colombo
කොළඹ දිස්ත්‍රික්කය
கொழும்பு மாவட்டம்

'The sojourn was tranquil,
the sojourn was sweet,
now on with the journey,
and Godspeed to all we shall meet.'
- An Ode to the Road, Dan Doughty

Tucked away down a litter-strewn back alley, behind a series of high-end hotels, my taxi came to a halt at a not-so- high-end hostel. Harsha, the pleasantly amicable taxi driver, helped me to lug my haul of hefty luggage to the door of a rather wilted looking property. I only had a selection of 5000 Sri Lankan rupee notes afresh from the airport ATM. I handed a bill over and thanked him. The driver's face beamed with merriment as he waggled his head uncontrollably from side to side.

A murder of crows glided above the rooftops cawing as the light of dawn broke. The air was already warm. I rang the buzzer on an intercom and waited. The buzzer was probably about the most modern aspect of the property. Its once white facades were now mottled and some of its windows were boarded up as a thick vertical streak of algae bloomed the five-storey property from top to bottom in an eternal leak; the place undoubtedly had a strong sense of abandon. A rat scurried past and vanished into a pile of bin bags; a round of high pitched squealing ensued - someone in there was getting their head kicked in.

The door abruptly buzzed and unlocked as I clumsily dragged my bicycle bag and duffle bag into an incredibly dim corridor. A bleary eyed man of whom didn't appear overly enthralled to make my acquaintance doddered ahead of me up a flight of endless stairs, where he would show me to my dormitory bunk. The old familiar smell of spilt beer, camembert, curried farts and a mystery infection loitered in the stale confines of the dorm. The quintessential olfactory products of any international hostel; a consistent smell that after many years of backpacking came to represent a home away from home - a kind of nostalgic denigration in a way.

I walked over to a crumbly and precariously poised balcony that overlooked a brick wall. It was hardly an inspiring view. I considered a nap, before a crow dropped down from somewhere above and landed on the balustrade that I lent upon. Non fazed by me it edged closer. I kept still until it was barely half a metre away. It tilted its head and a beady black eye scanned my face. For the better part of a minute we stared into one another; completely silent and completely still. Did it want food? My soul? To warn me of impending doom or perhaps to be my spirit guide? As ridiculous as it reads, I felt like it was trying to tell me something at least; but I just wasn't quite avian enough to work it all out. Then suddenly, from high above came the gruff caw of another crow. The trance was thus broken and the crow was once again bound to the sky. The city was the crows own to explore. And from that, I massed inspiration. Its message suddenly became clear - for beyond the brick and mortar that lay stacked before me, there was a whole new land for me to explore. My nap was therefore postponed with immediate effect, as my adrenaline surged to optimal levels. I needed to see beyond the wall. My Sri Lankan experience had already begun.

*

One is never too far away from a crow in Sri Lanka, just like one is never too far away from one of it's 1.2 million auto-trishaws. If you're lucky enough, one might even be able to enjoy the sight of a driver whizz either past or inconveniently directly through you, whilst he casually eats a bowl of cereal and makes a phone call to one of his homies. If you're really lucky, the driver might even be blind arse drunk or just plain blind; it is often very difficult to gauge the difference. For in Colombo, just like in its English sister city of Leeds (That's right, Leeds! Leeds! Leeds! That Leeds!), it is as if the pandemonium never ceases (Even more so if you step off the pavement). Some might even say that this is the appeal of Sri Lanka's executive and judicial capital. In a country with a population of just over 20 million people its capital is home to some 750,000 inhabitants. A vibrant city with a diverse mix of ethnic communities: Sinhalese, Tamils, Moors, Chinese, Portuguese Burgher, Dutch Burgher, Parsis, Bharatha, Malay, Kaffir, Bohra, Memon, Indian and various other expats from across the globe that have all come to call the city home. Every face in the metropolis helps to paint a picture of the island's history, and to some degree its future.

The roar of traffic was immense. The perspiration on my part, even more so. As I ambled along the pavement the accompanying architecture was as varied as the city's inhabitants. A variety of the modern, abject ruin and colonial past dictated the city's panache. Colombo, with its natural harbour has long been a chartered city for many a seafarers. With its wealth of spices, traders from all the ancient empires of China, Persia, Rome, Arabia, India and Greece did at some point in history embark upon the islands shores.

'Bom dia!' In 1505 however, trading diversified somewhat, with the arrival of the Portuguese. They struck a sort of deal with Parakramabahu VIII, the then King of Kotte, the Portuguese were thus allowed to set up base in Colombo and trade in cinnamon, a much sought after crop that could be found in abundance up and down the coasts of Sri Lanka. In exchange, the Portuguese were to protect the surrounding waters from foreign powers. The deal however turned out to be a dud for the locals - for as soon as the Portuguese had gained a stronghold on Colombo, they marched on to influence and muscle their way into other coastal territories of the island. And by 1593, they had virtually complete control of the coast. Rumblings therefore ensued in the Kingdom of Kandy - an area nestled deep in the islands rugged and mountainous interior. To the Portuguese, the Kingdom was a stubborn and impervious fortress. And to the Kingdom of Kandy, the Portuguese were a thorn that needed removing. Sooner, rather than later.

'Goedendag!' The Dutch Republic were only too pleased to play a part. In 1638, they signed a treaty with Sinhalese King Rajasinha II of Kandy, whereby for aiding the removal of the Portuguese, the Dutch East India Company (VOC) would get prioritised dibs on trade within the region. It took the Dutch until 1656 to jostle the Portuguese out of Colombo, and then a further 2 years to completely suppress them across the island. Those that were not slain, scrambled back into the waters from whence they'd came and headed back out west - where then, they were probably slain by the Spanish. Thereupon in 1658, with the Portuguese ousted and the Dutch in firm control of Colombo, it soon came to light that the Dutch had no intentions of handing back control; or sticking to the aforementioned signed treaty. And so, just like the Portuguese, the Dutch would rule the coasts of the island. The Kingdom of Kandy again, was quite rightfully pissed. Ceylon, as current day Sri Lanka was once known, would continue under Dutch rule for a further 156 years.

'Well, hello there sailor, lovely day for it old chap, wouldn't you say? Absolutely spiffing if I might say so myself.' Said the British in a roundabout way in 1796. Through years of war across land and ocean, the Dutch had become a weakened power, and through the French Revolution a Napoleonic France had finally ground the Dutch Republic into defeat. The British East India Company of whom at such a point had firm footings in India soon moved across the short stretch of the Laccadive Sea and thus ceded control from the Dutch to form British Ceylon. A name the island kept until 1948, when She was finally given her independence from foreign rule. The island as the world knows it today would then become Sri Lanka. In 443 years, over the course of four centuries three colonial powers had influenced these shores. These chunks of colonial history have left an indelible mark on the city's landscape.

I crossed a busy intersection to receive a mouthful of black as night trishaw fumes. On the other side of the road, one of the city's most iconic parks: Galle Face Green. A mile long sandy stretch of lawn extended before me, accompanied by a number of stalls that aligned a coastal promenade selling various snacks and gifts. People mingled, flew kites, laughed, dined and played. The Dutch once used the area as a strategic vantage point to lay out their cannons so that they could blast holes in the Portuguese Fort that sat poised to the north. When the British took control they had more of a recreational vision. The green being used for various sports such as horse racing, polo, rugby, golf, football and of course cricket.

A trishaw passed me by, it's driver asleep at the wheel.

To the south the Galle Face Hotel, a building that certainly wouldn't be amiss in a period drama. An elegant colonial shore front property dating back to 1864 that in the past had catered to the likes of Mahatma Gandhi, Prince Philip the Duke of Edinburgh, Princess Alexandra of Denmark, Indira Gandhi, Richard Nixon, Lord Louis Mountbatten and Sir Roger Moore.

I walked northerly along the promenade; a prickly sweat on my back as my shirt began to hug me more tightly. The Twin Towers of The World Trade Center and adjacent cylindrical Bank of Ceylon Tower jutted up from the central business district of Fort. Beneath them, colonial mainstays such Cargills department store, the Old Dutch Hospital and the Old Parliament Building. Street names and geographic locale were a mishmash of international fluctuation: York Street, Flagstaff Street, Mudalige Mawatha, Duke Street, Regal Terrace, Chaithya Road and Sir Baron Jayathilaka Mawatha.

Just off of the coast to the west of Fort, a series of ships dotted the ocean as large cranes towered high above. Closer inland a chain of trucks plied back and forth across a scruffy looking construction site kicking up waves of dust that cloaked their surroundings in a whirly mist of sand and grit. An evolving landscape of inner-city modernity as a new city was in the process of being birthed. A new city within a city: the Port City. The 665 acre plot is to be reclaimed from the Indian Ocean and will form the new financial district that will supposedly boast new skyscrapers, hospitals, parks, marinas, a beach, theme park and Grand Prix circuit. It is said that it will be able to house an estimated 80,000 people and see some 250,000 commute there daily to work and play. As I write, the state owned Chinese firm China Communications Construction Company (CCCC) had invested some £1.1 billion pounds into the project; the largest foreign investment in Sri Lankan history. All part of China's 'Belt and Road Initiative,' the modern day equivalent of the Silk Road that will no doubt see to it that the Chinese have an advantageous economic grip on the region. A huge and controversial investment that will see dredging ships scour the seabed for some 65 million cubic metres of sand. Ecosystems will be destroyed and coastal erosion will inevitably follow; in turn, affecting an estimated 15,000 local fishermen in the process.

Farther east of Fort and on towards Pettah, the streets begin to narrow like stiff, concrete arteries. From somewhere, a Bollywood banger belted out at eardrum knackering decibels. The red and white striped Jami Ul-Alfar Mosque that looks like a giant liquorice treat, captivates amongst the external hustle. As a whole, the buildings of Pettah were less grandiose; bunched together and seemingly dependent upon another. But, at the same time offered up their own unique and quirky charm. The level of commerce here became more coarse and intense as the din and hurrah of Pettah unfolded. The streets a riot of trade, where hawkers and punters haggled and jostled in what seemed like equal measures. From stall to stall a world of oddities and essentials unraveled: flip flops, handbags, backpacks, suitcases, whoopee cushions, cosmetics, fabrics, textiles, roof tiles, floor tiles, mobile phone cases, lightbulbs, barbed wire, bog rolls, fruit, vegetables, mystery snacks, adapters for this and that along with every kind of electrical and plumbing component and fitting you couldn't even possibly imagine, or even ever need to for that matter.

A trishaw driver razzed past and honked a horn at no one and everyone as men relieved precariously parked trucks of their produce and disappeared into the swarm of commotion.

I then stepped in a puddle and broke the crust off of something far from sanctimonious as a dark and ambient ooze washed over my feet.

> *Pettah was exciting,*
> *Pettah was alive,*
> *Pettah for me...*
> *was the place to be.*

These useless lyrics rallied around in my head as I worked my way through the masses. I told myself they'd be good lyrics in a rap song that I'll never produce. And thus far, I'd remained true to my very word.

South of the bus station, as manic as any other bus station across South Asia, is the Pettah Floating Market. A newly established build that consists of 92 stalls set along a cut of water linked to Beira Lake. More of a tourist draw with its souvenirs, handicrafts, local produce and upscale restaurant.

A short wander farther south saw me navigate my way to the waterside of Lake Beira. Dug by the Portuguese some 500 years ago as part of a crocodile infested moat system; in aim to protect themselves and their fort from the Sinhalese kings and their invading armies, that were all more than eager to see their heads sat on spikes. The surface area has shrunk over the centuries, from somewhere in the region of 0.64 to 0.25 square miles; largely in part due to various acts of drainage and land reclamation. Connected to a network of canals the lake was part of a system that carried produce across the city. The lake once lined with a ramshackle cluster of warehouses and dwellings. Sewage from the local inhabitants was often routed into the lake and thus an open cesspit materialised, giving the area around the lake somewhat of a bad name.

Yet, like all things modern day Colombo, the attraction of commercialism has superseded the stink. From the outskirts of cleaner, croc-free waters, skyscrapers edge their way up into the troposphere like overwatered glass sunflowers. New condos, hotels, a casino, an array of glitzy restaurants and cafes and the opportunity to ride a shitty swan pedalo all look to seduce Colombites and tourists alike.

A trishaw passed me by, its driver contently read a newspaper.

To the eastern shores of the lake's waterfront and another extravagant construction project neared completion. Rising up some 356 metres into the cerulean blended sky - a huge pinnacle in the form of a metallic pink lotus flower gloats. A cost of £89.5 million, the aptly named Colombo Lotus Tower has taken nearly 7 years to construct. At the time of writing, it was the tallest self-supported structure in South Asia and the 19th tallest tower in the world. If one ever happens to be disorientated or lost amongst the clustered streets of Colombo then this eye catching landmark is most certainly a definable way-marker.

At 5pm, the traffic approached gridlock. Police dictated the flow by blowing eccentrically upon a high pitched whistle and throwing their arms about in the air in a well choreographed fashion, like they were rehearsing for a part in a new Taylor Swift music video. A bigger surprise was the elephant that strolled past cloaked extravagantly in red with sequins of gold and silver. It was soon to be the Medin Full Moon Poya Day, where Buddhists across the country celebrate the Buddha's homecoming to visit his father, King Suddhodana of Kapilavastu; his first visit since becoming a Samma Sambuddha, the highest level of Buddhahood and therefore a fully enlightened individual. Many Sri Lankans visit temples during this time, where they listen to Dhamma teachings and flock to the sacred heartland of the country to trace the steps to the summit of Sri Pada.

In the well-to-do neighbourhood of Cinnamon Gardens, home to Colombo Town Hall, the Prime Ministers office, the National Museum, Independence Hall, Colombo Public Library and a bulk of foreign embassies and high commissions, I sought refuge in Viharamahadevi Park. A verdant inner city oasis of some 24 hectares, where the white noise of nearby traffic merges into a reliable hum. A golden Buddha keeps watch over Town Hall as folk take time out under the numerous shady bows of the park's Banyans. Dark clouds soon gather as a storm began to brew. The fresh spittle was initially a much welcomed refreshment. The monumental downpour to follow however, not so much.

As I emerged soggily from out of the western fringes of the park and headed back in the direction of my hostel, a trishaw would pass me by, its driver cruising at a steady 60mph casually lifted a dumbbell in one arm whilst taking a selfie with the other. I applauded him, as he modestly waggled his head from side to side.

Colombo - Kandy
81 miles

Through a maelstrom of chaos, I ambled out of the city's throbbing hub. A morass of trishaws, buses, motorbikes, jaywalkers, street dogs, crows and cricket balls lay in my wake. The law of averages dictated that I shouldn't escape the city in one piece.

During the previous evening at my fart-laden hostel, I'd unbagged and pieced my bicycle back together; pedals on, handles bars aligned, tyres locked in and re-pressurised, derailleur re-assigned, panniers attached. As far as I could tell it hadn't suffered any in-flight damages and early testing revealed that everything seemed to be functioning as a solid unit. Whether this was to remain the case as it had done through the 6,800 miles that took me around Japan some 4 years previously, remained to be seen. But having done me proud in the past I saw no reason not to once more ride my faithful Ridgeback into the unknown. If it's not broke, don't fix it.

The same principal applied to my cycling attire - whereby I donned the exact same civvies that saw me through my Far East venture: a navy blue moisture wicking t-shirt, some Umbro England shorts and a pair of velcro Sketchers. I either considered them good luck omens by such a point, or I was just a massive tight wad; I couldn't quite decide. But for certain, it felt as if I was more than hell bent on wearing them until all-out disintegration.

As I breached the outer reaches of Colombo, I cycled along some higgledy piggledy back roads through some lugubrious and forgotten looking suburbs; where I was met by a curious array of local eyes. Some waved, some hollered, some stared and some couldn't give a flying fuck.

The inevitability of the A1 to Kandy eventually beckoned; a road that was never destined to act kindly to that of a meagre cyclist such as myself, or to that of its chief engineer. In 1820, the construction of the A1, or Kandy Road was initiated by Lieutenant General Sir Edward Barnes, the acting British Governor of British Ceylon at that time. The 71.99 mile stretch was the first of its kind to connect coastal Colombo to mountainous Kandy nearly 500 metres above sea level. A road carved into the wilderness of the heavily forested interior of the hill country was no easy feat with 19th Century technology, or therefore lack of it. Alongside his work force of largely native employees, all manner of nasties awaited them and lead engineer Captain William Francis Dawson of the Royal Engineers. The swelling rivers were lined with crocodiles and the forests brimmed full of testosterone fuelled elephants and prowling leopards. And in the darkest depths, creatures of venom and little remorse lurked. Disease was rife and the soaring heat of day only exacerbated the struggle. Lives would inevitably be lost, including that of Captain Dawson himself; sources suggest that either snake bite or dysentery took him in the end. The Dawson Tower monument stands tall at the pass of Kadugannawa - as a memorial to his efforts.

My current feat was by no means an equivalent to the sweat and toil of Captain Dawson and his men, but it was in no uncertain terms, a ruthless and muculent slog. The sun was at its zenith; blazing and brutal. The heat - atrociously stifling. For the better part of 50 miles, a romp of heavy and continuous traffic flowed like a river of metal and rubber . In the mid-day climes the ascent simply put, was a savage and unrelenting bastard. But it was the price I would have to pay for my entry into the mountains of the much fabled, Kingdom of Kandy.

2. Kandy
මහනුවර දිස්ත්‍රික්කය
கண்டி மாவட்டம்

*'Honour to the Blessed One, the Exalted One,
the fully Enlightened One.'*
- Namo, Pali Canon, 800 CE

Downtown Kandy was a scene of pure carnage. The roads were swollen with traffic along a one way system that veered around the perimeter of Kandy Lake. Horns tootled and peeped in an orchestra of frustration as an inescapable gridlock took hold. I gingerly squeezed through the gaps where I could; much to the envy of the local trishaw drivers, of whom honked and waggled at me with dissatisfaction. But then they were seemingly honking and waggling at anything that had a pulse.

As I cast my eyes over towards the lake, I felt as if I were stuck somewhere between heaven and hell. People strolled leisurely around the lake where they chatted and laughed (possibly directly at me). A lady adorned in a vivid emerald green *sari* dined on some tropical looking fruit that was completely alien to me. On a stone bench a heavily hair-bunned backpacker took time out to scratch his or her testicle. Across the lakes liquid fern coloured surface the outline of the surrounding hills were elegantly reflected. The lake itself was by no means natural, having been artificially dug from a rice paddy by King Sri Wickrama Rajasinghe in 1807. Towards its middle lay a small island clad in cherry blossoms; a place where it was rumoured that the King's hareem once bathed and pampered themselves. Furthermore, it is said that the island has a secret tunnel that leads directly to the Royal Palace. Something that I can neither confirm or deny to be utter bollocks.

'HOOOONK!!!!' A big red bus disrupted my daydreaming and was evidently furious that the trishaw in front of me hadn't moved forward all of 0.4 millimetres. It was a gritty, slow and gradual affair, that eventually saw me thread my way through the humdrum and away from the lake and farther up into the hills to where my hostel were situated.

The smell of weed lingered in the air as a dog the size of a walrus lounged by reception. A half baked lad with dreads welcomed me and showed me to my six-person dorm; one that I could just about smell beforehand over the aromatic waft of marijuana that lingered due-diligently at the reception desk. It was partially full inside, the amount of fetid socks strewn across the floor dictated that there were potentially more than just six persons habituating the dwelling. But I knew from a historical stance that littered socks could in no way, shape or form be a solid indicator of such things. I saw two empty bunks and grabbed the bottom one. Across from me a bearded man with what looked like an upside down head lay on his bunk and watched

YouTube! videos. For the whole two days I was at the hostel he would remain cemented to his bunk. He nodded at me and I reciprocated. Another door opened in the room and my eyes lit up as a couple of blonde girls in barely existent panties and flimsy half-shirts came running out giggling and dripping fluid everywhere that I presumed was water. A topless, tattooed and semi-towelled brick shithouse of a man followed out soon thereafter.

'Fuck bro, Norwegian girls! Who knew??' Commented the 7ft something man in an Aussie accent. He introduced himself as Ali, and we shook hands. He wore his towel in a very cavalier fashion and I was slightly concerned that I might get a glimpse of what a real man looked like.

'Hey bro, you mind if I play some Fleetwood Mac?' Enquired Ali, after we'd exchanged with the small talk.

'Not at all bro, not at all!' I wasn't going to argue with him, there was always room for a little Fleetwood Mac in my life. Ali pressed play on his mobile device and the dorm was soon filled with a sweet, fervent zeal of a timeless music.

*

In Sinhalese, Kandy is known as *Maha nuwara*, meaning 'Great City.' It is the capital of the Central Province and with a population of over 125,000 citizens, the second largest city on the island, . A city that boasts a refined wealth of historical and religious significance to the Buddhist faith, that can be traced back as far as the 15th

Century; when it's first monarch Senasammata Vikramabahu ascended to the throne. For over three centuries, the Kingdom of Kandy ruled the Hill Country; a forbidden place to outsiders of whom the Kandyans saw with suspicious eyes. The kind of place where more often than not, invaders and colonialists were sent packing to the lowlands with more pieces of themselves than they'd arrived with. However, where the Portuguese and Dutch had failed, only the British struggled (1803) and then ultimately succeeded (1815) in their hellbent pursuit at world domination. And thus, the last independent kingdom of Sri Lanka was toppled, marking the end of a long line of Sinhalese Monarchs as Sri Vikrama Rajasinha was deposed and ceded by George III, the new monarch of then British Ceylon.

Yet, despite the better part of a century and a half of foreign influence, Kandy has managed to retain its deeply embedded religious and cultural heritage. So much so that in 1988 the sacred city was designated a UNESCO World Heritage site. I'm not entirely sure if those wheels were greased by the fact that in 1984 vast chunks of Spielbergs 'Indiana Jones and the Temple of Doom' were filmed here, but, I was more than interested in finding out what all the fuss was about. As was my new found 7ft behemoth Aussie mate Ali.

'Where you off to bro? Said Ali, as I sidestepped a sleeping werewolf in the reception area.

'I'm going to go and check out the Temple of the Tooth.'

'Cool bro, sounds shit! Mind if I tag along?'

'Sure man! Why not? Won't your Norwegian lady friends get jealous?'

'Nah bro, I got me a date with a German chick lined up for tonight, she's as fit as!'

'Oh ok, fair enough.' I think I took an instantaneous liking to Ali; there was a certain hearty charm about the big Aussie.

We had to pass a stringent security check to get into the grounds of the Sacred City. And for good reason, in the past it had twice succumbed to terrorist attacks. In 1989 there was a shootout between guards and the Janatha Vimukthi Peramuna (JVP), a Marxist-Leninist Communist political party. And then, in 1998 a series of suicide bombers from the guerrilla separatist movement of the Liberation Tigers of Tamil Eelam (LTTE) infiltrated the complex.

Ali and myself could only hope for a more tranquil visit as we were patted down, frisked and ushered fourth into the grounds of the Sacred City.

'That guard touched the tip of my dong bro,' claimed Ali.

'Do you think you're going to be alright?' I asked unconcerned.

'Yeah it's all cool bro, I'm from Melbs, I've had worse.'

Ali was still in his early 20's and seemed to be the perfect amount of unfazed as ideally possible. I envied that in a way. The bit where he always gets the girl and everyone wants to touch his dong, perhaps even more so.

It was crowded within the temple complex, and the heat seemed to scowl at us in exchange for perspiration. A throng of Chinese tourists swarmed past us like a human centipede as they followed a tour guide with a red flag atop a pole like it was a piece of bait. Every one of them, seemed to screech and shout in an abstract form of obnoxiousness that made it difficult to decipher whether or not they were elated or angry.

'So big!' Commented one lady, as she sized up Ali upon passing.

'Fuckin' dick,' remarked Ali, as he glared back at her.

It is said that when Lord Buddha was cremated in 543 BC, that his remains were scattered across the Buddhist realm and that his canine was considered one of the holiest of the holy, and that whomever heralded the tooth, possessed the authority to rule. Therefore the tooth became very much a sought after piece of real estate and a very un-Buddhist like war broke out across India in an attempt to attain this most prized of holy assets. The tooth relic eventually found its way to what was then known as Lanka, today's island of Sri Lanka. There it moved from kingdom to kingdom, before finally finding its place at the Temple of the Sacred Tooth, in the Kingdom of Kandy.

The smell of incense permeated the air as devotees offered prayers and donations. The room was grand in every sense. A decor of wooden carvings, marbled bollards and a disgusting amount of ivory adorned its confides. The centre piece a golden casket, where within six more caskets that dwindled down in size to where lay, the tooth of Buddha. So, you can't actually see it. But, it is in there, allegedly. And for me, I was content enough with this knowledge.

'This is bullshit bro.' Ali clearly wasn't satisfied. 'I wanna see the fuckin' tooth!'

'Erm...I just don't think you can,' I certified uneasily. Not entirely sure if Ali was going to kick off and cause a scene. It's hard only knowing someone for five minutes sometimes. They could literally be anyone. That's why after many years of being a sweaty backpacker I often find it easier to play the part of upside down head man back at the dorm. Although, I have little to no interest in watching YouTube! videos all day. RedTube videos? Well...then that's a different story - but let us not get sidetracked.

'Fancy a beer bro?' Ali looked bored.

'That I can do!' Now more at ease with the knowledge that Ali wasn't a complete psycho, as he too like me, liked to answer his conflictions with booze.

'Beer and Fleetwood Mac?' He suggested with an edge of inflection, as if the two weren't necessarily meant to go together, but by some form of preternatural intuition, we both knew that they did.

'Fuck yeah bro!' I endorsed and systematically encouraged.

3. Kurunegala

කුරුණෑගල දිස්ත්‍රික්කය

குருநாகல் மாவட்டம்

'One cannot drink porridge without getting some on his moustache.' - Sinhalese idiom

Kandy - Negombo
73 miles

Come morning and my head hurt. Placing my feet upon the ground and committing to vertical mode was painstakingly problematic for my brain's equilibrium. Across from me on a top bunk there was a mound of flesh. Some of it Australian and some of it either Norwegian or German, I couldn't quite decipher. I could barely remember the night before. But sometimes, just sometimes that's a good thing.

As I made my way to the bathroom I had to step over what looked like a mushed plantain in a rubber sack. Upside-down-head-man smirked before going back to watching his YouTube! videos.

I approached the sink and took a long, hard look at myself in the mirror. I looked wired.

Me: Who are you?

Me: That's for me to know and you to find out.

Me: Well how mature, how about grow the fuck up?

That, I declined to answer too, as I splashed my face with water and refused to look at myself again for a fortnight. Disgusting.

I knew that if I lingered at the hostel in this state, that it was only going to be a depressed and feel sorry for myself kind of day. Outside, dawn had barely broken, but already the air weighed heavy with the scourge of humidity. Regardless, I needed to make a move.

As I packed my belongings together, Ali immodestly worked his way down from his top bunk as naked as the day he was born.

'Ah what, you hitting the road bro?' he said, his tone almost disappointed.

'Yeah man, this hangover isn't going to burn itself off.'

'True dat bro, true dat!' He wandered over stark bollock naked. 'Gonna miss ya bro!' I went to hold out my hand but he wasn't having any of it. I got his biggest bear hug. He then grabbed a soggy looking towel up off the floor, slinging it over his shoulder, he made way for the bathroom. He stopped suddenly in his stride, something had triggered a thought worth a mention as he twisted his neck around towards me.

'She licked my arsehole bro,' said the big Aussie. In fact, I'd never seen a prouder looking Aussie in all my life.

'Oh cool...that's...that's nice bro. Thanks for that.' Was the least I could offer, the very least.

'See ya around town bro!' Sniggered Ali. And with that, he stepped over his bag of sins and departed for the bathroom. The bromance was over.

In the courtyard outside the hostel, I loaded my panniers up in a fit of sweat. The day had the potential to be a grind. But in my favour, I would be descending from the Hill Country and back down to the coast - with the intent to return to the hills from the east at a later date.

I wheeled my bicycle out onto the road, where I noted an Ayurveda centre next to the hostel. I wondered if they had a remedy for a stinking hangover. Alas, they were closed and therefore I was destined for the traditional approach of feeling like somebody had just taken a great steaming dump inside of my body. This was the way.

*

The descent from Kandy down to the dusty streets of the ancient royal capital of Kurunegala was a smooth and hassle free transition. A large Samadhi Buddha statue some 20 metres in height keeps watch over the city from atop a large elephant shaped hill. From all around a series of rocky land formations jut up prominently, like sentinels keeping watch. Many of them said to resemble various animals - such as the tortoise, eel, beetle, goat, monkey and most famously the largest rock of all - the aforementioned Elephant Rock. Athugala, as it is known locally, towers up 325 metres above the city. Local gossip dictates the story of a severe drought in the area, whereby the local animal populous were being held accountable by the thirsty locals for such a shortage of the wet stuff. Therefore, a witch was hired to turn them all into stone. Presumably and quite rightly so, she either couldn't live with what she had done, or she was a bit of a shit witch, as there also happened to be a 'Witch Rock.'

From Kurunegala, I traversed south westerly to the shores of Negombo. The roads at times treacherous and unforgiving. This however drove the devil out of me, i.e the alcohol. My senses sharpened as a matter of instinct, for if they did not, I'd have been getting shipped home to my loved ones in a Tupperware pot of mush and gristle.

4. Gampaha
ගම්පහ දිස්ත්‍රික්කය
கம்பஹா மாவட்டம்

'Your word is a lamp to my feet, and a light to my path.'
- Psalm 119:105

Negombo

With its plethora of evenly priced hotels, eateries and sparsely populated beaches, Negombo is for many often considered the more palatable option for arrivals and departures to and from Sri Lanka. I settled for the Silver Sands Hotel, a colonial build with an arcade of white washed colonnades and high ceilinged rooms with mosquito splattered walls. For my standards it certainly looked ritzy, albeit at the not so ritzy price of 3000 rupee (about £12). Partiality also played no part here, for there was even space in my room for my bicycle.

Whilst exploring the confines of my large airy room, I trod upon something that popped and soon became squishy. Lifting up my bare foot revealed that I'd accidentally stomped upon on a spider about the size of a well built puppy. I screamed a little and retreated - despite the fact that the spider at this stage wasn't likely to do me any harm. Alas, it felt almost instinctual for me to recoil in abstract fear, because to be quite frank, spiders scare the absolute bollocks off me. Something that I'd mostly, always held a trip to Australia accountable for. I still felt bad about indiscriminately murdering the big fella though, and wondered how I might clear up the mess. An unnecessary concern in hindsight, as within moments the cleanup crew had arrived. No, not Winston Wolf, much smaller - as a legion of ants found their way in through the gap underneath my bedroom door and dutifully marched across the threshold and over to the scene of the crime. There they got to work straight away, and took further to the act of disemboweling the sorry looking arachnid. They were soon to be carrying it away limb by limb back to their queen. It was as all over in the space of about 10 minutes; as if the whole ugly affair had never happened. It was a fascinating watch all the same, ants truly are a marvel. I was also now at least fully aware to what would become of me should I get smattered all over the road on this trip.

The Silver Sands backed onto the coast. A broad beach dotted with the occasional slob catching a few last minute rays, before departing to climes almost certainly less desirable. I trailed the coast south to downtown Negombo. The closer I got the more polluted the sands became. A wide selection of failed and rotten remnants of commerce littered the beach; where children rummaged for spoils. Nearby an old market place, alive with the raw grit of the hustle and bustle of commerce. For Negombo, trade is something of a systemic pastime. With a sheltered lagoon just to the south of the city, many a trading vessels have plied its waters over the years. The Sri Lankan Moors, of whom make up 9 % of the population of Sri Lanka, are said to have descended from 8th Century Arab seafarers, that once took to dominating the islands cinnamon trade in the area.

Through the city's central hive of motorised mayhem, I found part of the Dutch Canal. From the the time of the Dutch Administration to present day, the canal system that covers the better part of some 100km is still frequently used for the convenient transport of supplies and fresh produce.

As dusk encroached, I circled back to my hotel. Lightning blitzed the distant skies out to sea from where a contemptuous breeze rolled inland. I took it upon myself to relax on my balcony, with a hair of the dog and a mean dish of curry and rice; the staple of a nation. Moments like these are to be relished, for there is often a tomorrow of uncertainty. My situation as it were, of 'here today, gone tomorrow,' was however already beginning to feel like the norm; an invariably satisfying norm. The stress levels were down and the dopamine levels at an optimum. There were trials ahead of me that I knew for certain could make or break a person; trials all the same that I hoped to take under the wing of the proverbial norm - for there was after all, little other choice in the matter.

Negombo - Chilaw
29 miles

At the cusp of dawn, I was awoken by what one could only possibly describe as symphonic terror. It was 5:30am, and the orchestra from the Catholic Church next door to my hotel had decided to fire up the harmonics. It was an intense sound, not too dissimilar to that of the *Ave Satani*. And when I heard the guy in the room next door begin to vomit violently through the walls, it made me wonder if perhaps it was in fact an exorcism taking place. *I should probably get going*, I thought.

I couldn't have asked for better weather to start my days proceedings. The skies were clear and the humidity condensed by a modest sea breeze. I cycled along the dusty driveway of my hotel and turned left onto Lewis Place - a vast touristic stretch of road aligned with an abundance of hotels, guest houses, restaurants, bars and cafes. I passed the once so very vocal Holy Rosary Church; that now sat eerily silent. Negombo has the highest concentration of Christians in the country, and is the central hub for Roman Catholicism; introduced by the Portuguese back in 1505. The city today boasts some 25 churches dedicated to varying saints and martyrs, and is often referred to as the 'Little Rome' of Sri Lanka. Christianity (7%) along with Hinduism (12%) and Islam (9%) being minority faiths on this vastly Buddhist (70%) island.

Branching away from Lewis place, I ventured in a northerly trajectory, a direction I would now be headed in for the next 10 days. The roads were lively, but by no means malicious as I passed through a busy intersection at Kochchikade. Rickshaws darted about belching out ghastly clouds of jet black fumes whilst women adorned in beautifully vivid saris walked barefooted along the hot paved roads balancing heavy laden bags of produce upon their heads.

I crossed a bridge over the Maya Oya River, the supplier of water to over a million inhabitants before it feeds into the Indian Ocean. A network of mangroves interlaced with palms skirted the rivers breadth and trailed deep into the islands interior. Dark clouds of crows swooped overhead and seemed to trail the rivers course inland; dotting the landscape and making it appear like one of those old grainy collodion wet plate photographs. A wild land awaited them as it did me - where elephants roamed free and leopards stalked the shadows. A place where macaques swung skilfully through the tree tops and crocodiles lurked in the shallowly depths. Down there somewhere, in the hidden undergrowth, rare orchids sporulated in between the gaps of weaving vines as tough as steel. It was an island paradise that gloated all manner of fauna and flora; enough to keep any budding naturalist engaged for several life times over.

With a fervent passion I cycled forth, in an eagerness to explore the avenues that awaited me in a land all still so new to me. A new discovery around every corner. Everlasting memories being etched to my hippocampus. I was at it again. I'd jacked it all in for a life back on the road. I wasn't doing it their way anymore, I was doing it my way. I felt privileged and free, and so incredibly fucking grateful for it.

5. Puttalam
පුත්තලම දිස්ත්‍රික්කය
புத்தளம் மாவட்டம்

'Welcome to the jungle,' - Axl Rose

Grand mansions poked out of verdant pockets of jungle as I wound my way through a puzzle of roads to a coastal stretch that led me all the way to Chilaw. The road surface was a combination of paved, slightly paved, nearly paved, consideration of being paved and a bit of good old not paved. I'd pass though a number small fishing settlements, of whose tongue twisting names I could barely pronounce: Nainamadama, Wennappuwa, Kudumaduwella, Thoduwawa and Ambakandawila. In each village ramshackle huts lined the road, where the days catch was on display for all to see. Some of the locals waved at me as I cycled through as others looked on in abstract bewilderment. Stray dogs chased me and barked excitedly; yet when I stopped my bicycle they seemed to have nothing more to say. I overtook a grumbling go-kart disguised as a tractor, where children hitched a ride on its trailer. They all bellowed an enthusiastic chorus of *hello's* towards me, and much to their delight I reciprocated by hollering right back at them. The clear ocean waters mesmerised and the delicate salt laden air intoxicated. It felt right to be here, it really did.

By mid afternoon I'd arrived amidst the central hum and buzz of downtown Chilaw. A town with a diverse mix of ethnicity and religion that was once famed across the land for its pearl fisheries. I checked into a hotel on the outskirts of town. There was an inner desire to keep on cycling, it had been a refreshing day in the saddle; mostly straddling the breezy coast. But, I didn't want to overdo it, knowing full well that at some point, I definitely would overdo it.

I had myself a fish curry at the hotel and took a stroll down to the shore front. Whereupon I pitched a seat upon a sea wall. Next to me a litter of puppies fought and tussled amongst themselves as close by on an adjacent sandy field a noisy group of boys played cricket. The sky had become overcast, with fragmented lines of crimson that occasionally broke through. It soon seeped a hot and strangely soothing rain.

Chilaw - Kalpitiya
57 miles

After a hearty breakfast of pancakes and fruit I slunk down a back road and out of town towards the temple complex of Munneswaram. This intricate Hindu site with its symbolic fusion of lively paintings and sculptures dates back to 1000 CE, and is one of the five Pancha Ishwarams dedicated to Shiva in Sri Lanka. Followers believe that the temple was established by Rama, the seventh avatar of the God Vishnu, of whom once worshipped here.

Whilst parked up (and chained to a post with a 2 kg motorbike lock), my bike garnered a plenitude of local attention. I watched from afar to begin with as I exited the *kovil*. There was a lot of touching and gear shifting going on, but nothing malicious at play, mere curiosity. As I approached I was hit with a flood of questions: Where you from? How much bike? What your wage? Where's your wife? Do you have Facebook? An all round inquisitiveness that I would soon enough become accustomed too. I'd also get asked if I fancied swapping my bike for a local variant - a creaky old Chinese made one-speed wonder. A proposition closely followed by a cheeky smirk and a soft to medium head waggle.

Away from the temple, I ambled into rural Puttalam, along a quaint country road adjacent a lively wetland. Here, a large group of painted storks foraged, flushing out their prey with their spindly feet whilst swinging their bills from side to side in the shallow waters - with the hope of catching a fishy feast. In the rapidly accelerating heat of day a cow sought shade under a colossal banyan tree as a cormorant close by dried its wings high up on a tree branch. From somewhere a peacock complained.

The road wound around and eventually spilled out onto the A3 - a busy section of road connecting Puttalam and Colombo. It was a monotonous yet relatively hazard free ride north that I'd traverse for the better part of 10 miles. The most endearing aspect being the sight of a local man on his push-bike, sweating and panting his way towards me. Just as he'd managed to draw level with me, his face beaming with pride, he pulled out a packet of smokes and offered me one. I felt somewhat rude declining him, especially after his sincere efforts, but one mustn't break that habit of a lifetime, not now. He seemed none too offended though, as he waggled his head a little from side to side before he ceased pedalling to light up and invest in a conversation with a sweetcorn hawker. All along the road were pit stops and various convenience outlets. A multitude of trucks pulled over in the dirtied lay-by where their drivers collected their morning tea and puffed away on cigarettes; the days duties never too far away.

I'd soon veer from the A-road and onto a heavily potholed backroad seemingly under construction. Various sections were being filled in by tractors and then consequently steamrolled. It was slow going and I'd often have to wait for the workers to finish a section before I was ushered past. As I remained static, the heat made itself known; a sticky membrane coated my skin as reams of sweat dripped down from my brow and onto my handle bars. When I wasn't waiting around it was again a meticulous process of weaving around the craters trying to dodge the rim breakers and spoke busters. Concentration on this section was imperative. Yet, clearly concentration wasn't enough, as before I knew it, I began to notice a wobble in my rear wheel.

Pulling over into the shade I took a look. I'd lost a spoke.

Practically, this was an easy fix - if however, it wasn't for the fact that the broken spoke was on the drive side of the bicycle, meaning I'd have to remove the cassette to get at it. For that I would need a cassette removal tool and chain whip, both of which I'd foolishly left at home like a wanker. I know, I know! I can already feel the heat from all you crackerjack grease junkies out there reading this, *'Like 'OMG!! I can't believe he forgot his chain whip! What a wanker!'* I do declare that on the face of it, it was a shameful act. Alas, it was what it was, a little bit of a pickle, but nothing to get too worked up about…yet.

I cussed a little to myself before taping the loose spoke to another spoke so that it wouldn't cause any damage to the rest of the wheel. I figured I'd be able to ride on it still for a little while at least. But then, what other choice did I really have? Finding the tools for the job or someone that knew what they were doing with the rare and illusive Ridgeback Tour was going to be a tricky one. Especially as I chartered further north and away from the country's capital. And so, just a few days into my journey and I'd already acquired some additional food for thought. Amidst such a quandary, I also found myself getting awfully hungry. I had to press on - and hope that I not lose another spoke.

Farther along a broken dirt track I cycled through a small number of chirpy backwater villages. Passing a school it must have been break time when somewhere close to a hundred or so children came flocking over to cling to the school railings, to wave and to shout at this strange and disgustingly sweaty looking outsider. I waved back and gave them a hearty 'hello' and in countenance they all went absolutely berserk; jumping up and down like batshit crazy mentalists as they congratulated and hugged one another at what I guessed must've been a relative anomaly of sorts.

At a T-junction I was eventually gifted a well paved road. Right offered me Puttalam, or left Kalpitiya. I chose the latter. A road that ranged through a narrow spit of land some 30 miles long and 5 miles wide; on the map it looks like Sri Lanka is giving the finger to neighbouring India. It channels between the Indian Ocean and the 126 square mile Puttalam Lagoon. An area that boasts an abundance of surrounding marine life, from whale sharks, turtles and dugongs, to large pods of dolphins as well as both blue and sperm whales. And with its blustery gales it had also become somewhat of a Mecca for kitesurfers.

Before long I was slaving forth through what felt like the straightest and most endless road in the world. Hemmed in by a vast contingent of baking hot salt-pans, where the heat haze that for so long had seemed to burden the horizon had now come to greet me. Here, the brackish waters of Puttalam lagoon are manoeuvred into large clearings that eventually dry off to form salt crystals. An almost inexhaustible resource to be exploited and a well sought-after commodity, yet an unbearable place to exist as a human. In this place, the very idea of some shade was seemingly an illegal proposition.

I found myself struggling. Really struggling. Under a cloudless sky the heat radiated profusely and it all felt like a little bit too much, intense even. Shit me, I was fucking melting. And then that feeling that began to creep up at the back of my mind, what was that? Regret? *Well you can fuck right off lad, there was no place for regrets on my watch.* Mind over matter was evidently going to be the key here. As I looked across this inhospitable landscape that gleamed so bright that I could barely open my eyes. The heat, it dizzied and my throat became parched. I took a hit of water from my canteen; it was warm and tasted sour. I think even my shadow had melted away; singed to the bitumen some half a mile back. Overhead, I could just about make out the darkened outline of a soaring eagle, or was it a vulture? Perhaps waiting around to pick me off.

Amongst this desolate and baking hot hell I came to a broken and sordid looking bus shelter. It looked out of place in such a harsh environment. But it did have one thing going for it: shade. The concept of a short break out and away from the heat stroke inducing climes was an appealing one. I propped my bicycle up against the shelter, kicked some plastic bottles and crisp packets out of my path and dumped myself upon a stone bench. I let out an exhausted sigh and closed my eyes for what must've been about 1.4 seconds.

'Hello sir,' came a voice that for a second felt like a stranger that had just fallen into my head. All the same, I nearly shat myself silly as I opened my eyes to a slim man with bushy black hair that hovered over me. He had a face that looked disconcertingly like a growl. He held out his hand that nearly went directly into my mouth before introducing himself, 'I am Romford!'

'Romford?' My voice rising an octave in bewilderment as I took his hand. *Romford? Surely not.*

'Yes sir, Romford, please to meet with you.' And as we shook, the growl swiftly converted to a smile. It was then that I knew that I wasn't fucked. I'd been to Romford before, a place of few smiles.

'I'm Daniel, pleased to meet you too...sir,' I eventually replied, my brain slow, yet full of wonder. *Romford?? How an earth did that happen?*

'Bye Daniel,' said Romford just as suddenly as he'd greeted me.

'Err, yeah ok, bye Romford, take care mate!'

Romford took a glance at my bike as he stepped back out into the sun scorched landscape. 'Very good,' he declared, turning back to inform me. I gave him a two thumbs up salute. He looked confused for a moment, before he reciprocated with both thumbs and a courteous waggle of the head. He then walked out of sight and around the back of the bus shelter. Meeting a bloke called Romford in the middle of a blistering salt-pan was about as bizarre to me as it probably was for a bloke called Romford meeting a bloke on a bike in a blistering salt-pan.

There was a giddiness that came over me as I drained the last of my acrid tasting water and decided to push on. No point lingering once one is out of fluids. As I got back in the saddle the heat as merciless as ever, I scanned for my new friend. But Romford was apparently long gone.

I felt like complete shit as I rode on. But, would eventually manage to wean myself away from the salt-pans before heading off-road and towards the small coastal settlement of Kudawa. There I found a tree that offered up a modicum of shady relief. I stood under it, until I only felt like a little bit less than complete shit - a mere shit perhaps.

A broken dog watched me as I cooled off. He saddened me, with half of his muzzle hanging off; his lost and desperate eyes searching for something unbeknownst to anything this earth could cater for. Flies persistently hassled his wounds as he scratched out at his scaly mange ridden flanks. I tossed him a biscuit and he ran scared. He'd clearly never felt the kindness of a stranger before, perhaps he'd never felt a kindness from anyone.

I pressed on towards the outskirts of Kalpitiya along a busted old track, amongst a marshland of wind turbines and brackish pools bordered by a hardy collection of low lying scrub. Veering closer to the coast, the skies out to sea began to darken and threaten a storm that would ultimately fail. I had some trouble finding my nights accommodation, as my hands were so completely sweaty I couldn't even swipe the screen on my so called smart phone so that I might unlock it to check my GPS location. Whilst cussing away to myself that it was somehow Samsung's fault that my hands were too clammy, a juniper coloured 4x4 pickup truck pulled up alongside me. Its blacked out window wound down and a sensual blast of cool air escaped before being lost instantly into the surrounding mugginess. A long haired man with a pierced eyebrow asked if I needed help.

'Sun, Wind Beach Kite Resort?' I queried.

The man simpered slightly, as if the task was far too easy for him, before pointing towards a gathering of palms some 20 metres away with a big, bold sign that very clearly read "Wind, Beach & Sun Kite Resort." 'You're already here bro,' he confirmed.

'Ah, right...yeah...thanks for that.' I said, feeling like a bit of a dick. The kindly stranger waggled his head cheerily, wound up his window and drove on.

I had to get off to push my bike into the resort, as the sand soon formed deep ruts around my tyres thus bringing me to a halt. The resort itself was simplistic in its laid back beach vibe atmosphere; merely a series of rattan beach huts made from palm, and a small restaurant in which to cater for its guests. Plus the mandatory lazy tones of Jack Johnson wanking off in the background somewhere.

An elderly lady of whom spoke little English ushered me over to my beach hut and told me that a dinner buffet was at 8pm. In the meantime I guzzled about a litre of water before any sort of logic and cognitive aptitude could return to my person.

Looking at my odometer I had doubled the mileage when compared to yesterday - and that was with the heat, that I always knew was going to be one of my biggest obstacles. Well today, that factor suddenly became a reality. If I wasn't to keel over, I would need to take it easy, somehow. And essentially, stay hydrated.

I took a quick glance at my broken spoke and decided that it was a job for another day. Instead, I walked down to the largely isolated beach and watched a few kite-surfers mill about guilelessly off the coast; the wind more than there for the taking.

At about 8pm I attended the restaurant buffet where I was accused by a French couple for eating too much chicken. I ate one more wing to justify the situation. 'Now I have,' I confirmed. I then went to bed. French friends are not compulsory. I think I read that somewhere.

Kalpitiya

A vast swathe of the morning was spent trying to leverage the cassette from my rear wheel. The hotel owner and his friends had also soon gathered around with a collection of archaic tools in an effort to try and save the hour. But alas, there wasn't a hero amongst us. With bloodied and grease ridden hands we all had to accept outright defeat. The hotel owner suggested a trip into downtown Kalpitiya to find a saviour.

Downtown had no particular nuance of interest, say unless you had a fine appreciation for flawless anarchy. Noise competed with noise for the sake of noise whilst the highway code was systematically exploited to the point of lawlessness. Pissed up rickshaw drivers tore about in battered vessels honking their horns at one another with symbiotic hostility. Through a tightly packed market place, mopeds muscled through the crowds with boxes precariously balanced to the front, rear and sides of their respective rides. As trucks and buses that neared all out dilapidation tore along the sidewalks in some sort of frenzied bloodlust. I was fast beginning to learn that this was all quite standard and to be expected. If you wasn't nearly flattened on a trip into town in Sri Lanka, then something was massively out of place. And, if you were to make it home without incident, you would surely be branded a bonafide liar.

Searching amongst the chaos did however reveal a fair share of bicycle mechanics about town. The scenario normally consisted of an elderly man out front, crouched low as he rotated an inner tube in a small tub of water - searching for that elusive tear; a rusty spanner never too far from his side. Behind him, his office: a grease splattered cuboid shaped room with a piled up mountain of cluttered rubber and mystery metal.

As I approached the first mechanic, he looked up at me from his dirtied tub of oily water with what appeared to be a combined semblance of both surprise and fear. A surprise and fear that seemed to exacerbate when:

A: I ignorantly spoke in English, and

B: I pointed at my bicycle in general.

His head instantly wobbling with dismissiveness, wishing me away as it were. He clearly wanted nothing to do with me and my paranormal bike from realms unknown.

The next few shops were exact carbon copies of the first. I'd always draw a crowd of onlookers that would touch and hold my bike (and shift the bloody gear levers!), but no one was quite willing to commit to the responsibility of fucking up my bike.

I took a fizzy pop break outside a small convenience store, where I began to lose face in resolving my technical glitch. Whilst taking a ridiculously massive gulp, I noticed a teenager in a light blue *kameez* just across the street. He was pumping up a bicycle tyre. Behind him, a darkened room of unevenly stacked metal, accompanied by both new and used tyres. A youthful wealth of mechanical experience echoed from within. Unable to multitask, I choked on my fizzy pop and spaffed most of it down my 2001/02 season West Ham shirt. I wheeled my bicycle across the street and noticed that the young man's hands were decorated in oil; the markings of a saviour no less. I showed him my predicament and he showed me a complete lack of reluctance, as he took the bicycle from me and had its tyre whipped off faster than one could say 'Llanfairpwllgwyngyllgogerychwyrndrobwllllantysilio gogogoch.' And then what soon followed was an incredibly scary ordeal - whereby the young mechanic took to attacking the rear hub with a hammer and chisel. For the better part of 30 minutes he hammered away as I sweated in the shade, slightly teary eyed. I just couldn't help but notice that it wasn't quite the same technique used by the ginger Canadian lad on YouTube! at all. Occasionally, I felt compelled to tell him not to worry, and that if he wasn't sure then to just leave it, *just leave it mate, it's not worth it!* But no, with his discreet mannerisms that spilled confidence, he somehow gave the impression that he was firmly in control of the situation. Unlike me, he wasn't sweating a bead, or perhaps I was just doing all the sweating on his behalf; it certainly felt that way. *Let the saviour do his job Daniel,* I soliloquised uneasily to myself. Then I thought, how would I like it if somebody came to the pub and told me that I wasn't drinking my beer properly? Well yeah that's right, I wouldn't like that at all and I'd be rightfully pissed, on top of already no doubt being quite leathered. And so, I sat back and sweated in silence and let the beauty of a young mechanical mind play out before me. I also closed my eyes.

CRACK!!! My eyes abruptly opened. The hub was

suddenly disembowelled; ball bearings having flown everywhere. Some of them hitting the compulsory crowd of onlookers that had since gathered, and some of them to this very day doubtlessly still in orbit. By this point I could't really tell if it was sweat or tears running down my cheeks. I closed my eyes again and bit my lip nervously. After some minutes had passed I plucked up the courage to take a another peek back at the scene of the slaughter. Surprised to note, that my spare spoke had since been attached and that my hub was being packed with copious amounts of grease and fresh ball bearings. The young mechanic was very meticulous about this part and took his time adjusting it before he was happy. Another 20 minutes had passed before the hub and cassette were back on the wheel. He then tensioned the spokes, trued the wheel and placed it back on the bicycle. Job done. And henceforth, the prophecy was fulfilled, the Saviour of Kalpitiya had performed before me, a small miracle. I'd had my initial doubts that I forthwith felt a bit bad about (still do), but like all good saviours, he came through with the goods. For what use was a saviour if they didn't come through?

    I settled the bill, which came to a pittance, so I greased the young saviours palms with some extra gratitude so that we might both part ways with the feeling of triumph. My bicycle was good to go again, and for that matter, so was I.

Kalpitiya - Eluwankulama
47 miles

As the crow flies my destination of Eluwankulama (easy now!) was only about 8 miles away - across the Dutch Bay of Puttalam Lagoon. Some small scale and mostly shoddy investigative work as to whether or not I could attain a boat to the other side of the lagoon came up fruitless. Alas, my bike can't swim and so thus I was forced back south. Yet, with the wind in my sails I was soon enough rounding the southern end of the lagoon and connecting up with the long road north.

The heat was as relentless as ever, and I'd noticed that the leather of my handlebar grips were beginning to melt. As I passed through the district's administrative capital of Puttalam with it's borderland vibe I was overtaken by three youths bunched up on a single moped. They turned to goad me on, teasing me to try and catch up with them. I shook my head and feigned having a heart-attack. It was solid bants. They laughed and left me to melt my way north.

To the side of the road a billboard advertised elephant repellant. The absurdity of it made me chuckle to myself. And as the land appeared to get drier by the mile, I took to thinking just a little more about that billboard. *Elephants sometimes turn humans into mince. You know that right Dan? Shut up, idiot, just keep cycling.*

On the outskirts of Wilpattu National Park I'd

navigate down a botched dirt track to find the non-signposted Wilpattu Jungle Lodge. A couple of dogs chased me down the driveway amongst some towering palm trees and a small mango orchard. Stopping outside a derelict looking building with whitewashed walls and a corrugated roof, I leaned my bicycle up against a palm tree. The lively dogs jumped up and nuzzled me like old friends as I crouched down stiff-legged to pet them. A quick glance around the place and I could see that there were no other signs of life.

The door to the derelict building was wide open and so I walked in; the dogs followed. To say the place was a no thrills establishment would've be deemed somewhat of an understatement...of the century. The double room was unkempt, the walls rotten and the floors dirtied as if they hadn't been swept or mopped in a generation. The roof of the mosquito net was loaded with a bountiful array of invertebrate corpses. The bed sheet itself no better; at the very least it probably hadn't been washed since 1993. The room looked like it belonged in an art exhibit at the Natural History Museum. Without a shadow of a doubt, the place had fallen upon hard times. But, was it still a place that I could call home for the night? I cast my mind back to some of the decrepit hovels that I'd once stayed in down Khaosan Road. Probably.

I stepped out onto a porch and sat upon a rickety looking yet somehow inviting chair. The building situated close to a crest, overlooked an impenetrable looking swathe of jungle. A cool breeze presented itself that soothed my sweat-sodden body and rustled the surrounding tree-tops. The moment was undeniably blissful. From out of the bedroom somewhere a tired looking puppy appeared yawning. I picked him up and put him on my lap. With minimal fuss he soon fell asleep. The other two dogs that had initially greeted me upon my arrival had also declared a siesta, as they threw themselves down sloppily onto the floor of the porch. I didn't really blame any of them, there was a certain sleepy ambience perusing the vicinity that afternoon, one that came on strong and seemingly refused to take 'no' for an answer. The concept of a nap suddenly became irresistible. I closed my eyes for a moment.

'Ah, I see you've met Washington?' Boomed a voice, boomingly. And as I opened my eyes a completely bald and burly man began to make his way up the short flight of steps and onto the porch.

'Err…Washington?' I was still slightly confused, how long had I been out.

'Our newest addition to the family,' he pointed to the puppy on my lap, of whom was now fully awake and padding his paws up and down and wagging his tail excitedly. The large man picked up the little dog and nuzzled him.

'He's an orphan you know,? They think a leopard got his mother.'

'A leopard? Are there many….in the area?' I queried,

slightly bothered.

'Oh a few, you normally don't see them though.' He kissed Washington on the snout and put him down, before he clumsily ran over to play with the two bigger dogs. 'And those that do…' he paused, 'don't normally live to tell the tale.' He looked at me somewhat coldly. I felt my eyes widen. The large man burst out laughing, 'But you'll be fine,' he assured me as he held out his hand, 'I'm Zev.' With all the scary leopard talk I'd began to sweat quite tellingly again as I held out my sticky mitt to shake hands.

'You did well to find the place,' said Zev, apparently aware that his accommodation is not a place so easily found - or one that perhaps wants to be found.

I pointed at the dogs, 'your furry friends showed me the way.'

'Ah yes, yes, they are good dogs,' at that very moment one of them went to run into the bedroom. 'FUCK OUT!!' Bellowed Zev… bellowingly. The dog fucked right out. 'So, that will be your room,' he pointed towards the rooms broken interior. 'How many nights would you like to stay?' I looked back into the room and noticed that since I'd left the door open at least another few kilos of random insects had found their way in. One such bug was about the size of a jacket potato with weird claw hands protruding from its butt - where it seemed hellbent on biting chunks out of the furniture - with its butt.

'Probably, just the one night I recon.' I said, turning

back to Zev.

'Very well, but there's lots to see and do around here, you should stay a week...or perhaps ten weeks?' He picked up a stick and threw it and the dogs chased after it. 'Or, you could just stay forever,' said with his back to me almost making me shudder.

'Err...I'll probably just...' Zev turned back to face me, a sinister little smirk on his face, the guy was obviously a bit of wind-up merchant.

'I'm just joking Daniel, Sri Lankan humour, with a touch of New Yorker.' He then told me to grab a towel and invited me down to the local river for a swim.

'Yeahhh? The river?' I responded with some mild hesitance, crocodiles instinctively springing to mind. It was probably another gag I thought. But when I saw Zev go to his bungalow and return with a towel in hand, I knew that this time he was serious. I tentatively fetched a towel; my bowels had started to churn somewhat and my mind started to flap. *Your face is going to get gnawed off by crocs mate, and that winky you grew all by yourself? Well, you can kiss that shit goodbye too!*

'Oh come on man, that's enough!' I said.

'Everything ok there Daniel?' Queried Zev at my sudden outburst, at myself.

'Oh yeah, sweet, all good mate, lets err...go get gobbled up shall we?'

As we walked through varying scrub towards the Uppu Aru, Zev told me that he'd spent 25 years working as a banker in New York. At the end of which, he had decided that his love for nature and a longing for his homeland had become overwhelming, and so he decided to return to Sri Lanka and open up his little guesthouse in a rogue patch of jungle. He seemed very knowledgeable about the local fauna and flora as he pointed out various species along the way. The dogs ran up ahead, coherently aware of the designated route. Young Washington however had to stay at home, for he was still far too young for late-afternoon jungle adventures.

Before long, we had made it down to the river. The water was dark and far from innocent looking. Anything could have been lurking down there in its mysterious depths. Zev belly-flopped right in and vanished, clearly no fucks given. I found myself beginning to wonder whether or not he had just woken up a sleeping family of reptilian flesh manglers before he thankfully resurfaced. 'Are you not coming in?' He questioned.

'Erm...yeah but, like....what about the crocs?' I queried, like a nervous Nellie.

'Ohhh it's ok, just as long as you stay on this side of the river!'

'Okaaayy…'

'Anyway, why are you so worried about the crocs? Tomorrow if you plan to cycle through Wilpattu, the elephants will be a much bigger problem for you.'

It was then that I began to think about all the crazy animals that could ruin a persons day on this densely populated tropical island country of some nearly 21 million people: Elephants, leopards, crocodiles, bears, sharks, flying snakes, vipers, pit-vipers, cobras, pythons, kraits, tarantulas, scorpions, centipedes, fire ants, bullet ants, giant hornets, and that good old family favourite, mosquitos. I compared these concerns to those of my own densely populated island: gnats, fly agaric and chavs. I felt slightly ashamed. As for the locals, the majority of them would go about their daily lives unscathed. Incidents however were just seen as a way of life. If I was to traverse this country like I so intended, then I would need to get over any hang ups of getting mauled, maimed, ripped, lacerated, squeezed, impregnated or eaten alive. And so thus that neutralisation process needed to start at around about now.

I waded gingerly into the cool, dull water. It was somewhat refreshing. The dogs sat and watched from the bank; they obviously knew better.

'You know, I've only ever met one other guy that went to Wilpattu with his bicycle,' he paused for a moment to think, 'he was British too in fact.'

'And, how did he get on?'

He looked me over and issued me a stern look. 'I never heard from him again.'

We both laughed. Zev was a funny guy. A funny, funny guy. I think I liked him.

'But, on a more serious note, I actually didn't ever hear from him again.' The laughter stopped dead in its tracks - like a trampled cyclist on the side of the road.

During the night an overly eager army of mosquitoes hounded me, squealing like rabid freaks from the outside of my mosquito net; desperate for the taste of blood. From outside, a cacophony of insects whirred, screeched and whined. A pack of dogs roamed someplace distant - howling deep into the night. A cat screamed in distress and a peacock joined the party. I heard heavy laden footsteps ludicrously close by, accompanied by snuffling. Obviously somewhere out there, there was a monster on the loose, obviously. *Welcome to the jungle*, I thought.

Eluwankulama - Mannar
62 miles

'I guess I don't need to worry about the sharks too much today though right?' I said jokingly to Zev as I saddled up.

'Daniel, this is Sri Lanka,' he stopped momentarily to pick up Washington, who was amidst losing a fight to one of the bigger dogs, 'anything and everything is possible here.' He ripped into a contagious bout of laughter, his naked belly jiggled up and down like jellied meat. I'd miss that hearty laugh.

We said our farewells and I cycled away down the driveway, the dogs in chase all the way up until that invisible barrier that marked the edge of their territory that only dogs being dogs would know about.

From the village I trailed the asphalt north for a mile or so before the road returned to dirt. I soon came to a naval checkpoint that marked the entrance to Wilpattu National Park. The young, pre-pubescent looking officer manning the barrier looked at me somewhat bewildered as he raised the peak of his cap to scratch his head. A white boy on a pushbike was perhaps a first for him. He looked around for answers but it appeared that all of his colleagues and seniors had deserted him. In perhaps what could've been deemed a panic decision he waved me through. Both of us uncertain as to whether or not I should be riding my bike through Sri Lanka's largest and oldest of National Parks. A quick Google search pulls up a contradictory bunch of answers to that equation, but ultimately left me with the impression that I could cycle the road through the park, but it wasn't overly advised, because of all the bat-shit crazy wildlife that could potentially fuck me up.

Ahh, it'll be alright, I told myself, trying abysmally to put my overactive imagination to rest.

Past the checkpoint a short ford presented itself. About ankle deep so I was forced to take off my trainers and walk across. At the other side an elderly man in an immaculate white *kurta* appeared. His beard was scraggly and his eyes were wild, and quite frankly scary. As I took a seat on a wall to dry my feet and put my footwear back on, he looked me up and down and then scanned my bicycle as if trying to absorb everything in order to forget nothing. He then looked back at me, his eyes bulging. There was something about him that suggested that his mind had perhaps stepped out for lunch (for a few years!). He then pointed to the road ahead of me, 'jungle!' He declared, with a slightly eccentric twitch of his neck. I'd obviously mistaken the concern on his face for menace, but that still didn't stop him from being a slightly unnerving character.

'Yeah…it'll probably be alright,' I assured him, trying my best to be jovial in the odd heat of the moment. His bloodshot eyes shot me a glare, he looked wasted. I wondered if he had been on the toddy: a local delicacy whereby sap is derived from the coconut flower and allowed to ferment - in order to become mind bogglingly alcoholic.

The man again pointed to the road, but with an added emphasis this time on being slightly more aggressive, 'JUNGLEEEE!!!!' He roared like a manic preacher.

'Okey then, well that's enough of you.' I promptly shuffled into my saddle and left him to trip balls by the jungle ford. I didn't look back, not once, but his eyes were definitely burning a hole in the back of my head.

It wasn't long before the road would most certainly became that of jungle; as a fortress of scrub and thorn aligned the heavily rutted track. Occasionally the bush peeled away to reveal a vast fertile oasis of lush grassland and natural lakes known locally as *willu* - a name that forms part of Wilpatu, meaning 'Land of

Lakes.' For the most part, I was all alone on the road. Yet despite the scarcity of traffic, it was still considered a public road, and roughly once an hour an Ashok Leyland public red government bus would ply past, sparing my life by sheer millimetres whilst kicking up waves of dust and debris before leaving in its wake a wall of noxious pollutants. As my journey continued around Sri Lanka these buses would soon enough become my arch nemesis. Always and without fail they were loaded to maximum capacity and to traverse at anything less than about 80 mph was a disadvantageously deplorable concept. Their drivers were systematically ruthless, often whacked out of their minds on betel nut, they drove with such reckless abandon that they quite often tested the limits of how close speeding metal can get to the delicacy of live human flesh. Without fail, a customary lump would rise in my throat upon their rumbling approach as the seat of my saddle was impinged with moderate quantities of fear gas. They were never not terrifying.

A couple of mongooses danced across the road ahead of me and into the undergrowth. As I stopped to observe, I came to another opening through the prickly bush. A vast wetland lay sprawled before me. Some a hundred or so metres out a small flock of egrets waded its shallow waters close to a huge grey boulder. The boulder moved with a slow gait and casually swung its elongated trunk and flapped its large depigmented ears. *Fuck me, an elephant!* My brain as late to the party as ever, as my heart skipped a beat in both shock and awe at the spectacle. I remained static and observed for sometime as the solo big boy meandered slowly along, casually minding his own business.

The Sri Lankan Elephant is the largest of the three subspecies of the Asian Elephant. Population estimates put it at somewhere between 6,000-7,500 individuals. It is reckoned however that the population is in somewhat of a free fall in recent times, largely due to habitat loss from urbanisation and deforestation, that in turn has led to herd fragmentation. This places stress on both elephants and humans, as they both compete for resources to sustain their livelihoods. More often than not, during the cover of night, elephants will stray away from parks and into nearby farming settlements, where in a single night their wholesome appetites could devastate an entire crop. Conflict usually ensues, and each year some 150 elephants and more than 50 people are killed in such incidences. None of this particularly crossed my mind at the time, as an unnecessary necessity decided to take an abstract stranglehold upon me. I started to rustle about amongst my panniers like a fuckwit in order to find my camera. By the time I'd found it and pointed it at the big guy and got that all important shitty shot, I'd noticed that his huge ears had pricked up and he appeared to be looking my way. I shot a glance over my shoulder to see if he was perhaps looking at somebody else. Some other fuckwit pointing a suspicious looking black object at him perhaps. Nope, he was definitely looking right at me, and as we all know, an elephant never forgets (especially one that has perhaps taken a bullet in the past). *This is probably exactly how people get fucked up by elephants* I thought. *No, this is exactly how idiots get fucked up by elephants,* I concluded. I whispered a meek inconsequential apology towards the hefty proboscidean and slowly lowered the camera and slipped away - discreetly chuffed in the knowledge that I had just in fact seen a wild Sri Lankan elephant. And that for me, was something just a little bit special.

For a farther 20 miles I continued along a chiefly trashed and in places completely washed out road. It was tough going, the heat as usual failed to let me off lightly. I could taste the salt upon my lips as I perspired terribly.

Evidence of a healthy stock of elephants continued to emerge as I breached the road further north. Huge piles of dung christened the brightly hued red dirt track like great stinking termite mounds. Then eventually, as the dense scrub began to peter out, a paved road returned to the fold, this marked my entry into Mannar.

6. Mannar

மன்னார் மாவட்டம்

මන්නාරම දිස්ත්‍රික්කය

'The owl is small, but its voice is loud.' - Tamil proverb

As I cycled further from Wilpattu, I noted a vast number of newly established buildings that clustered the sides of the road. Each one an exact carbon copy of the other: lime green walls and red tiled roofs with the words 'JASSIM,' written across them. Many of these homes belonged to the displaced - victims of war, of whom had lost everything. If their homes were not destroyed then they were quite simply taken. Reports suggest that it became common place for deeds to suddenly go astray through a combination of mysterious and illegitimate circumstances. Thus many thousands, mostly Tamils, were left effectively homeless. It was quite often the civilians that would bare the brunt of the brutalities of war; losing everything that they possessed and all that was so dear to them, including that of their loved ones. People were frequently maimed, tortured, raped and murdered or just quite simply 'disappeared.' The displaced would end up living a hopeless existence, for years stuck in disease ridden camps set up by the government. Yet post-war, through donations from humanitarian charities such as the Jassim Charitable Foundation, residents have been able to start a life over - a life that during darker days would never have seemed possible.

On the opposite side of the road from me, an elderly lady sat on a chair in the shade. She stared fixedly into a rogue chunk of jungle that encroached upon the edge of her property, I dared not think of the things that she might've seen out there.

As I struggled through the settlement into a stiff headwind, a group of enthusiastic young boys came running over and started to jog by my side; all smiles, all heart. A couple of them placed their hands upon my back and gave me a running-push in order to help me along through the prevailing gusts. I thanked them in kind. Most of them were probably too young to have experienced the war, but doubtlessly in some way, they like many, were surrounded by the wounds of its aftermath.

I continued to wrestle north-westerly towards the A14. From there, a nearly 2 mile stretch of causeway connects the mainland to Mannar Island: Sri Lanka's largest island at 50 square miles. It was late afternoon as the low lying sun twinkled competently across the surface of the Indian Ocean. I was surprised to share the road with a pack of stumpy looking wild donkeys as they casually strutted along flicking their tails about to keep the bothersome flies at bay. Introduced centuries ago by Arab traders from Somalia, these once domesticated animals were seen to be hardy and well adapted to the local arid terrain. Able to carry heavy loads and ferry locals across town. However, in the light of modernity, trucks, buses, motorbikes, rickshaws and the likes, the use of donkeys for manual labour had fallen into decline, and thus most of their employment had dried up. Today however you'll mostly find them skulking about the streets of Mannar, rootling through mountains of disposed rubbish or rubbing their hinds up against aged baobab trees.

A wealth of life habituated Mannar Town upon my arrival at the end of the causeway. A blend of exotic spices and exhaust fumes occupied the air in a town thats general razzmatazz almost seemed well defined. Restaurants with their gaudy signboards began to fill up as the working day came to a close. A procession of uniformed students with textbooks in hand marched along the sidewalks as a noisy rabble of motorbikes and their three wheeled counterparts competed for space on the roads amongst the potholes and curious donkeys. From somewhere, a church choir sang.

As dusk settled in, I wound my way along a network of dust choked and poorly lit backstreets. I'd happen across 'The Good Luck Palace.' Not one to shun a fine piece of good luck, I brought my wheels to a halt.

On reception stood two identical twins dressed in identical attire. Blue shirts, black trackies and side-partings to match.

'Hi lads,' I said.

They stared back at me, both of their faces void of expression. I wondered if when they blinked if they did so at the same time. But they never seemed to blink, not ever. In fact, they didn't really seem to do much of anything apart from stare. Which made proceedings a trifle awkward.

'Erm...any rooms?' I put the palms of my hands together and feigned putting my head down to rest.

The staring continued, immensely.

'Is...err...mum around?' I queried, 'Dad perhaps?'

'YES SIR?' Shot out an exceptionally loud voice from so close directly behind me that I wondered for a second if I had not just been violated.

'Woah, Christ on stilts!' I declared, very nearly betraying the fabric of my undergarments. I turned to face an exceedingly large framed man of whom's eyebrows I could only really describe as mythical hairy slugs.

'GOOD EVENING SIR, WELCOME,' he held out a hand and we firmly shook for a ridiculously long time.

'Oh hello there, I was just asking the lads if there were any rooms available?' We continued to shake hands as I gesticulated with my spare hand towards the reception desk, where just sheer moments before the twins had once stood. The twins had since vanished. Of course they had.

'YES SIR, CERTAINLY,' he finally stopped shaking my hand and began to walk towards the now lad-less reception desk. 'ONE PERSON SIR?'

'Err...' I looked around, still slightly miffed that the lads had managed to just vanish into thin air. *Where the fuck did they go?* Before suddenly realising that a pair of mythical hairy slugs were winking at me with some mild concern. 'Oh sorry, yes, just one person, thanks.'

'AND HOW MANY NIGHTS SIR?' The bushy browed man looked into a ledger and ran his finger across the page.

'One, I think.' I might just be able to survive that I thought.

'PERFECT SIR, THE BOYS WILL SHOW YOU TO YOUR ROOM' he roared as he pointed to an entrance down a hallway, where the young lads had suddenly appeared, looking like a lad version of The Shining twins. *How did they do that?*

I followed them along a hallway, where the amplified echo of my footsteps created an absolutely unnecessary melodrama. The lads walked side by side all the way, at a consummate pallbearers pace. And then, in unison they both pointed at a blood-red door. I shuddered a little as I pushed the door open and entered the room within. Inside, a windowless box shaped room, a small single bed, a rusty fan, a light that flickered incessantly and something disgusting and squidgy looking in the corner that looked like it needed help. Perfect.

'Ok ,thanks lads,' I turned around to an empty hallway. 'Lads??'

They were gone. Of course they were gone.

I'd somehow arrived at the Sri Lankan version of The Overlook Hotel. I shut my bedroom door and locked it, and for extra measure piled my bags up against it. It had been a long day in the saddle and I really wasn't in the mood for the full Stephen King experience.

Mannar Island
41 miles

Inside a just short couple of miles, I found myself sweating from every pore and orifice that I had available to me. It was barely 9am as the sun methodically baked everything within its ballistic glare. I found it hard to believe that the giant gassy bastard was 93 million miles away from earth, as it felt more like a mere 9.3 metres away.

I was headed west down a higgledy piggledy road of bumps and holes, to the farthest reaches of Mannar Island. The distressing A14 scarcely populated along this stretch; a feral donkey here and there munching on some thorny scrub or a local on his creaky push bike equipped with a fishing rod as he headed to the coast to catch his lunch. Peculiar however, were the great balls of shit rolling down the road of their own accord. *Ghost poop?* I thought. Although on closer inspection it turned out to be dung beetles, shifting what had to be somewhere between 40 to 50 times their own bodymass. By using the powerful spurs on their hind legs, they roll the poop up into balls that they then either feast upon, or use to lay their eggs in. But what makes poop so lush to these beetles? Largely its the grasses and undigested materials in the dung that when fermented provides the beetles with a nutritious dose of protein-rich nitrogen infused poo juice. Lovely!

In Talaimannar, the A14 terminates. A small road shoots off further west, where I came to a slather of beach aligned with fishing shacks. There, I sought shade as the heat was becoming impossible. Finding a small cluster of palmyra trees close to Adam's Grave; an Islamic site believed to be the graves of both Adam and Eve. Inside the green walled compound, two elongated mounds lay side by side covered in green cloth. One 40ft long, said to be that of Adams, and the other 38ft long, belonging to Eve. The first man and prophet on earth is also named after the 18 mile shoal of sandbanks that effectively connects Mannar Island to Rameswaram Island in the Indian state of Tamil Nadu. A crossing that was once used heavily by refugees as a means of escaping the war torn island. It is said that the prophet Adam crossed this bridge on his pilgrimage to Adam's Peak in the central highlands of Sri Lanka. Yet, this is where a conflict of interest between the religions is interplayed. In Hinduism, the crossing is known as Rama Setu,whereby a series of stepping stones were placed by an army of monkey's sent by God. Therefore allowing Rama to cross from India to the then named Lanka, and retrieve his kidnapped wife Sita from the sinister clutches of the demon king Ravana. Jesus at this point still refuses to comment on the whole debacle.

Geographically however, the bridge is considered a broken up tombolo - a spit of land that once connected the two countries, dividing the Gulf of Mannar to the south-west from the north-eastern Palk Strait. Overtime, either due to the accretion and rising of the land and/or the breaking away of Sri Lanka from Mainland India, the tombolo has separated and broken apart.

For all intents and cycling purposes, I'd come to the end of the line with Mannar Island. It was time to head back down the A14 to Mannar Town.

TWANGG!! Another spoke gone. A donkey stood next to a signboard advertising Calpol brayed jovially. He/she no doubt thought that I was a funny fucker as I jumped off my bike to commit to a solid bout of profanity. At this rate I was losing a spoke every 100 miles. My spare spoke collection wouldn't be able to compensate for such a below par statistic. Thankfully, this time the spoke wasn't on the drive side at least, and therefore made it an easier fix once I got back to my hotel. In the long run though, losing another spoke so early on was a lingering concern.

The Shining lads awaited me upon on my return to The Overlook Hotel. They stared at me as I booked another night at reception. They then stared at me as I fixed the broken spoke on my bike. Later, across the street from the hotel at a restaurant where I went for a lukewarm curry, they stared at me from the gates of the hotel as I ate. And as I slept, behind a heavily barricaded door, somewhere out there, they continued to stare.

Mannar - Vavuniya
54 miles

I left at dawn, just after the muezzin had finished prayer. The climes tepid and approachable. I was chased through the backstreets by a wily pack of dogs, much to the amusement of a small assemblage of fishermen making their way to the causeway with handfuls of fishing nets. Across the stillness of the ocean a hazy mist rose across its surface as the sun edged up and over the horizon; soft and golden.

Back on the mainland, I continued east towards Vavuniya along the A14, surrounded by a lush enterprise of rice paddies; the country's main staple and second largest crop produced after that of tea. Within the hour the cool mist began to burn away as I hooked north and away from the main road. A white and blue archway with a circular stained glass window at its centre depicted the Virgin Mary; this signalled the jungle road to Madhu, where one will find perhaps the holiest Catholic shrine on the island. A shrine that is not only an important pilgrimage to Catholics, but to other respective faiths of whom all come to pay their courtesies and seek blessings from the statue of 'Our Lady of Madhu.' The statue was brought deep into the jungle in 1670 and kept a secret from the then ruling Protestant Dutch, of whom had banned Catholicism and had set about persecuting its many followers across the island. Alas, trouble still managed to find its way to

Madhu. In the 1990's as the civil war raged on, the church was declared a neutral zone and would go on to harbour thousands of Tamil refugees. That was until November 1999, when it was shelled in a conflict between the Sri Lankan Army and the The Liberation Tigers of Tamil Eelam. Both blaming one other for the atrocity.

Today, the Portuguese style church painted a brilliant blue and white, sits somewhat majestic amidst the jungle. The grounds are kept spick and span with a series of caged golden statues that depict varying scenes from the bible.

I wheeled my bike along and watched a small group of pilgrims pay their respects. I wondered about having a quick word with Our Lady myself, to see if she might ask the Almighty to bless me with a lovely little rain shower later that afternoon. But then equated that to a bit like going to ER with a paper cut, the Heavenly Father probably had bigger fish to fry. And, as I began to pedal east along a dusty secluded track farther into the depths of the jungle, I couldn't help but imagine that very conversation in my head.

God was up in his heavenly kitchen, or what he liked to call 'The Board Room.' He was frying up a pan load of scallops, when the Blessed Virgin Mary walked gracefully into the room through a doorway made of cumulonimbus clouds. When not trading in cryptocurrency she did odd jobs for God. She was currently armed with a clipboard and pen, with business clearly in mind.

'Ah Mary, how lovely to see you. Who's up first? Want a scallop?' Said the Lord.

'No, no I'm good thank you, I've just had sushi.' Replies Mary promptly, before waylaying directly into a recital of prayers from the Lords earthen children that had accidentally slipped into the spam folder; desperate prayers that sought help and divine guidance through the darkest of times.

'So, first up, Jimmy from Wisbech.'

'Hmm…Wisbech, didn't we sign that place over to the Dark Lord?'

'No, no we didn't, that was Tottenham.

'Ah Apologies Mary, my bad. Anyway, I digress, lets talk about Lil' Jimmy, I like that kid. What's up with him today?'

'Well, he just wondered if you could perhaps unshackle him of a burden or two?'

'Whatever for?'

'Well, on top of a mischievous bout of nits, he's become quite addicted to eating ants ,' said Mary quite sternly.

'Ants you say?'

'Yes sir, ants.'

'Hmm…I see, well let's relieve him of those ghastly nits then shall we? He can keep eating the ants though. They're a fantastic source of protein I'll have you know, exactly why I put them there!' God adds a bit more ghee to his frying pan and takes an exuberant whiff at the sweet aromatic blast that suddenly fills the room. 'And who's next?'

Mary ticks a box and continues. 'Up next, we have.....' she pauses and begins to shuffle a bit uneasily in her heavenly sandals, 'I'm afraid it's that Doughty bloke again.'

The Great Lords face twists slightly as he pokes harshly at the sizzling pan of now quite well done scallops before him.

'Hey, did someone say my name?' At that point Jesus walks into the kitchen and removes a piece of cold pizza from the fridge.

'Ah, well if it isn't sleeping beauty himself? How's the job hunt going?' Snarfed God, quite pleased with his wit.

'Dude, you're such a buzzkill.' Jesus picks off a curious strand of ginger hair from his slice of pizza and walks out the room carelessly, hitting his halo on the top of the door frame in the process. 'Ah man, I hate this thing!'

The Heavenly Father releases a heavy sigh. 'And what exactly is Doughty's problem now?'

'He says it's a bit too hot, and a spot of rain wouldn't go a miss. Just to tie him over until he gets to Vavuniya.'

'Oh good Lord, what have I done?'

God draws his scallops away from the hob with disdain and pours them into the middle of the Atlantic. He'd suddenly lost his appetite. He then walks over to the fridge and grabs a six-pack of Stella. 'If your want me, I'll be downstairs turning the heating up.'

'You stay away from that Dark Lord you hear me?' Shouts Mary after him,'he'll only lead you astray!'

But it was too late, he was already gone.

Back on earth in a completely non-fictional environment (to the best of my knowledge), I'd realised that the heat of the day had quite clearly started to make its mark. I was parched with a hint of delirium - doing an absolutely terrible job at both staying hydrated and keeping Christianity in a favourable condition. I gulped down the rest of my water and continued my sweaty journey east into what felt like eternal jungle. Safe however in the knowledge that I'd decided not to waste Our Lady's and the Divine Lord's good time.

7. Vavuniya
வவுனியா மாவட்டம்
වවුනියා දිස්ත්‍රික්කය

'There is love in friendship. Friendship is greater than life. The one who wins the heart of a friend, he has won the world.'
- Lord Krishna, Mahabharata

I arrived early afternoon in the vibrant Vavuniya. A town seen as the gateway to the north, that surges with trade and commerce. The only hotel I could find was a rather plush looking affair that seemed to be in the midsts of catering for a wedding after party - well dressed folk strutted about eating, drinking and spilling their way to a good time. The concierge seemed uncertain to begin with as to whether or not there was actually a room for me - as she barked and hollered at various colleagues, of whom eventually came to the conclusion that there was in fact a room available on the top floor.

'The Presidential Suite?' I enquired. The concierge delicately waggled her head and smiled, to which I took to be an acknowledgement of my tepid British humour.

By this stage in the book you may have noticed a lot of head waggling going on, the Sri Lankan head waggle is in its own definition a cultural trait. Deciphering it however is an art form in itself. Considered a figure of eight head waggle as opposed to neighbouring India's side to side head waggle, there are apparently different intensities for varying scenarios and marks of acknowledgement and gratitude. Some are subtle, blink and you'll miss it, others sincere and delightful, whilst the intense and drawn out ones are generally a bit awkward and occasionally farfetched.

I reciprocated the head waggle and the concierges smile began to broaden, before she barked some voracious sounding commands at three defenceless porters; of whom all seemed quite frankly scared shitless of her. They helped me with my bags and panniers and stored my bicycle in a back room before showing me to my quarters for the night. For $10 it was a grand room, in fact the best I would habituate during my travels around Sri Lanka. I somehow felt in over my head though, having the choice of three queen beds to myself, a reliable WiFi connection and a digital television with cricket on every channel. And to top it all off, I found a beer in the fridge. I couldn't believe my luck.

Fast-forward three sips later and I was wasted and thus decided to call it a night. For what was about to come, I'd need that rest.

Vavuniya - Jaffna
106 miles

Just north of Vavuniya, lay the Vanni, an area that covers some 2,950 square miles. Of that, 1,600 square miles is dense jungle. Its name derives from the Tamil word *"vanam,"* meaning "forest." The area is effectively a buffer zone between the north and the south, and during the civil war was a hotbed of violence and conflict that waged aggressively for almost three decades.

From the A9, I trailed north-westerly. The white noise of Vavuniya soon filtering away. I passed through a succession of smaller settlements: Kaddaiyarkulam, Thavasiyakulam, Mullaikulam and on to Iranaiiluppaikulam, where I came to a crossroads. There, a young boy slowly led a herd of cattle along a dusty, sun baked road. A man close by was parked under the shade of a tree where he snoozed on his motorbike. A pace of life that at at one time would have been seen as quite unprecedented. A signboard with a USAID logo emblazoned upon it read 'Building the Resilience of Returnees.' A white walled building with a red tiled roof sat aptly behind it. Again, this amplified the plight of the displaced in the region.

It was also here, in this remote pocket of jungle that an all female Tiger training camp once operated. The female forces made up nearly one third of the LTTE. Far removed were they from the archetype of being the doting domestic housewife, or the coming of age daughter. Here, women and girls as young as 12 were conscripted, trained in guerilla warfare and taught how to systematically slay their enemy. All before being sent off to the frontline with an AK47 and a vial of cyanide around their necks known as *"kuppie."* For it was taught that there was no honour in being caught alive.

From the crossroads, I headed due north towards Moondru-murippu, and deeper into the heart of the Vanni. I soon found myself very much alone, pedalling farther and farther along a narrow red dirt track. A glance at my mobile phone would soon inform me that my network operator didn't cover these parts. I'd officially gone deep jungle. And for that, I was ever so slightly nervous.

8. Mullaitivu*
முல்லைத்தீவு மாவட்டம்
මුලතිවු දිස්ත්‍රික්කය

'Necessity has no law.' - Tamil proverb

I passed remote buildings that stood as the husks of a violent history; ravaged by time and war. Walls bullet riddled and scorched black. Roofless properties, shelled and wrecked. Nature invariably strong-arming its way into the buildings very foundations like a concrete eating virus, squeezing in through cemented cracks and climbing through blown out windows. Each home carried with it a story, mostly lost, yet mostly obvious.

At Mallavi, a T-junction saw me re-engage with a brand new paved road, one that if I followed easterly would smoothly and no doubt courteously deliver me back to the A9. A deviant instinct from within however saw me cycling down another curious looking jungle pathway. To the entrance of the path a wonky looking shack with a corrugated roof; a place where one could buy drinks and snacks. I stopped by to grab a bottle of water and a couple of samosas. In the process of doing so a man approached me. He had a tall and gangly frame with a face that was harsh and weathered. He pointed to the path before me and simply said the words 'no good!'

'Oh...really?' I said, not quite sure how to respond, yet trying my best all the same to sound like a genuine idiot.

The man responded with a small wag of the head and a disturbed frown. Unfortunately there was enough vagueness there for my nativity to override the mans recommendation. I wondered if not briefly about the substance of those simplistic words - *no good*. Why? And in what context? Shoddy roads? Wild animals? A fallen tree? A burst water main? Hippies? Nothing me and my trusty steed could't handle, surely.

'Well, thank you anyway. But, it'll be alright.' Those famous last words; words that so often in my life have spelt absolute fucking disaster. I never cease to amaze myself about just how exactly 'alright' everything will be before the inevitable all out proverbial shit hits the fan.

The man waggled his head and his frown thickened. *Be alright.*

I peddled on, ignoring the sound advice of a stranger. I'd mostly regret that.

I was much further afield before my sun-scorched being could do a little more thinking again about just what might lay ahead for me. Mines? Rogue agents? Bandits? ….insurgents? Oh, bother. It was too late now however, I'd committed. Turning back upon myself is something that I'm ridiculously stubborn about. And one day, it will undoubtedly lead to my own undoing, for that much I am certain.

After a while I gained some company. From out of the scrub a young, bearded man in a blue shirt rode his bicycle barefooted. We greeted one another but spoke little, as it soon became clear that there was an obvious language barrier between us. But, reading between the lines he was off to Grannies house. We cycled comfortably and care free side by side for a good few miles, before he slowed down and pointed at the road ahead, 'dangerous,' he warned. A feeling of trepidation drew closer - that was the second warning I'd had.

But I'd have to remain stubborn, for it was the idiots code, the only code I'll ever know or need. One that admittedly I don't always appreciate, but I'm just not one to break a habit of a lifetime. There's no trouble until there's trouble. And at that moment, there was no trouble.

I thanked the young man as he turned away and headed down a dark and narrow jungle path, that to me, looked decisively dangerous.

I stopped momentarily and glanced at the path ahead of me. The horizon was like an oil painting that was melting and fusing together under the extremities. I sighed a little nervously, and continued to pedal the lonely path ahead. The surrounding jungle with its foliage thick and barbarous was eerily silent as a lump crept into my throat about the size of a natterjack toad.

About 10 minutes went by before a motorbike suddenly crept up beside me. Its rider a skeletal looking man in an all white garb. His hair silver and matted, his eyes bloodshot and from his mouth he drooled a dark curdy residue which I took to be *betel* nut; he was clearly inebriated. He began to talk to me in what I presumed to be Tamil. Naturally I had no idea what he was saying. I tried to politely remonstrate that I didn't understand, before his tone got decidedly more salty, as he rattled on some more in an intimidating manner - shouting and shaking his fists at me somewhat accusingly. Then suddenly he seemed to break off mid-sentence and just stare at me; as we both continued to ride along side by side in a tempestuos silence. His eyes cold and subfuscous. I looked away from the confrontation and continued to pedal. I didn't really know what else to do. When I look around and see the plenitude of smiles that had so far and so frequently greeted me on this journey, to suddenly meet someone so disenfranchised came as somewhat of a surprise. Not that I expected of course to be loved, lorded or adorned everywhere I went. Alas, that caring hospitable nature I'd experienced thus far had in this neck of the jungle forthwith perished.

   The man goaded me to look back at him. I refused. He then barked something uncouth towards me, before spitting a wholesome wad of *betel* nut juice at my feet and going on to cut me up with his motorbike as he tore away from me - leaving a trail of dust and confusion in his wake.

What the fuck was that all about? I pondered rather unsettlingly. I hoped that whatever the issue, that that was the end of it.

   I continued for another few miles before I saw the

man again. He was waiting by the side of the road with three assailants. I could feel them all staring at me as I slowly passed. I continued to look directly ahead, paying them no heed. *If I ignore them, maybe they'll just go away.* Their motorbikes thereafter soon fired up. My heart drummed and my stomach fluttered. I sweated a little more. And as the motorbikes gained upon me, my nerves became a little raw, but I strived to remain equanimous. I'd need composure here. They came with two motorbikes; two men to each vehicle. Coming up from the rear, one bike would settle directly behind my back wheel, whilst the other went ahead of me and slowed down trying to force me to a halt. There mannerisms clearly dictated to me that I had no reason to stop and that they had no reason to stop me. Not here, in the middle of the jungle anyway. I would most certainly be easier prey if I did. And if they wanted that, then they'd have to physically make me, which if they had absolute reason to do so, then they would surely have done so already. I weaved to the side and made it difficult for them to close me down or cut me up, using a sort of pedal and weave technique. Someone barked a frustrated order and the motorbikes then quickly drew up either side of me. The motorbike that traversed to my right was driven by my unsavoury *betel* nut chewing pal, his menacing eyes constantly leering. The man sat behind him spoke.

'Why you here?' He demanded interrogatively.

'Holiday. Just, cycling around Sri Lanka.' I pointed

ahead, 'meeting a **friend** at the **A9**.' Two buzzwords there that I felt important to name drop: A 'friend' told them that I wasn't completely alone and the 'A9,' knowing that in the general direction that I was headed I should at some point again be reunited with it (How far away I was from the A9 at that very moment however was a big fat unknown!). But figured by bullshitting the knowledge of my bearings that they would at least know that I wasn't completely lost. Little did they know, that as a rule of thumb I often actually preferred to get completely and utterly lost. But for the current concept of getting fucked up in the middle of the jungle... well, suddenly that was something that I wasn't so interested in bragging about. That kink had rapidly diminished - there and then.

The interrogator translated my words to the drooling driver, before falling silent. The drivers gnarly leer continued for what felt like a 30 second eternity. Again, he abruptly spat *betel* juice in my general direction and shouted at the other motorbike driver still riding close to the other side of me. Both bikes then fell away and receded back into the jungle from whence they came.

I let out an incredible sigh of relief, and with a tremendous surge of pent up adrenaline began to pedal furiously in the direction of the busy A9; never once looking back over my shoulder. I gritted my teeth together in anticipation of another encounter - perhaps more motorbikes, more men. It never came.

There was more to this tale than I'll ever really know.

I'd clearly stumbled upon a patch of jungle that made me a questionable anomaly. Rightfully so, maybe? The fact of the matter is Sri Lanka aside, people disappear every day, often without a trace - some of them travellers. But I was forewarned and customarily felt like a bit of a naive pudding-head for not having heeded to the now sound advice of various strangers earlier on during the day. I'm needless to say deeply thankful though, that outside these mild hostilities nothing overly malicious took place and therefore really, this wee yarn becomes a nothing story. Just one with questions that I'll never truly be able to answer. For undoubtedly, there was something going on. But, I'll take that over the possible alternatives. Whether or not on the day I played my cards right, or just got really lucky - I can't say. However, I'm certain that if these men from the Vanni genuinely wanted to stop me, then I would have been stopped. It certainly makes one think more wisely about one of man's greatest dangers... man.

9. Kilinochchi
கிளிநொச்சி
කිලිනොච්චි

'There is no instance of a nation benefitting from prolonged war.' - Sun Tzu, The Art of War

Closing in on Kilinochchi and the military presence was noticeably beefed up. Armed soldiers walked the streets as a concession of bulky green trucks chugged up and down the boisterous A9; a road that quickly evolves into an ostensibly endless drag of commercial enterprises. In their fight against the Sri Lankan government for an independent state, the town became the administrative capital and former stronghold of the LTTE. Here, the Tigers had their own banks, postal service, police force, judicial system and TV station. The town today, despite falling back into the hands of the Sri Lankan Army some 9 years previously, still wields a steely final frontier ambience. The air still slightly fraught with an undercurrent of lingering historical malevolence that once bloodied these streets.

Adjacent a manic intersection, I stopped to observe the 'Bullet & Flower Victory Monument.' A large golden bullet, more on par in size to that of a torpedo, sits embedded in a huge cracked slab of concrete. Above it a golden lotus flower; a symbol of peace. And atop further still, high up on a pole, flew the national flag of Sri Lanka, which hung limply in the halcyon yet clammy air.

It was late afternoon and I was tired and sweaty. The thought of finding some digs for the night was more than enticing. Jaffna was still another 40 miles off and I'd never make the journey before the cover of night. Plus, the day had already been strenuous enough after my jungle caper. Accommodation however, despite its obvious presence in the town, was more of a challenging task than I had anticipated. Each respective hotel manager would greet me with a dubious look, before going on to inform me that they had no rooms available. After several of these such failed attempts I took this as a sure sign that my journey was destined to continue into the night.

To the north of town I stopped to buy some deep fried mystery snacks from a street vendor; an elderly Tamil lady with a kindly face. When I handed her some meagre coin she contentedly loaded me up with a little extra mystery fodder. I waggled my head in approval and thanked her as she responded in kind. I'd need all the energy I could muster now; for the day (and night) was about to get a lot longer.

Across the road from this transaction lay one of the towns infamous landmarks and final bastions in the closing stages of the civil conflict: a huge fallen water tower. As the Sri Lankan Army piled on the pressure, the LTTE were forced to retreat from Kilinochchi. Yet, just before they left, in a final act of defiance the separatists took out the towns water supply. A low blow in a significantly dry zone whereby its inhabitants were heavily dependent. All throughout the hostilities, both sides lay accused of committing the most heinous of atrocities. Atrocities from conflictions that were seemingly taking place even before the emergence of a full scale civil conflict.

It was upon independence from British rule in 1948, that the then parliament of Ceylon passed a controversial "Citizenship Act," which thereby stated that any Indian Tamils, of whom at the time made up about 11% of the population of the country, were denied the right of citizenship. Many of these Tamils were brought in under British rule from the South Indian state of Tamil Nadu, where they came to work on tea, coffee and rubber plantations. And thus, in a country that many considered their home, they were overnight effectively declared stateless. Eight years later in 1956 and the "Sinhala Only Act" was passed. Sinhalese was sworn in to replace English as the sole language of Ceylon. Again, this caused a furor amongst the second largest ethnic group on the island: The Tamils; of whom spoke Tamil. Then in 1958, a pact that gave Tamils more autonomy was abrogated. This in turn led to outbreaks of ethnic violence. And as the years passed, frictions typically mounted. A ban would be put in place to restrict the import of Tamil language media to the island. And then in 1971, the "policy of standardisation" was introduced, which meant for Tamil citizens to gain entry into university they would need to gain higher grades than that of the country's Sinhalese citizens.

Inevitably clashes bridged a gap between the the minority Tamil population and the dominant Sinhalese. It was in 1972 however, that political frictions shit the proverbial bed. Ceylon would change its name to Sri Lanka, in an effort to distance itself from its colonial past, in doing so the government also made Buddhism the country's official religion. The majority of the Sinhalese were Buddhist, the Tamils however were largely Hindus. This was a sizeable catalyst in the country's civil unrest and in the north gave rise to various Tamil separatist movements and insurgent groups. Yet, there was one group of distinctly hardline lobbyists, that in 1976, led by one Vellupillai Prabhakaran, rose up to make a global name for themselves: The Liberation Tigers of Tamil Eelam, commonly referred to as the LTTE, or the Tamil Tigers. A movement of freedom fighters that sought for its own independent state.

In the early years a number of assassinations of politicians and government officials were frequently exercised. The shooting of the Jaffna Mayor Alfred Duraiappah in 1975 being carried out by Prabhakaran himself. Gradually, the violence escalated, and in July of 1983, the Sri Lankan Army was ambushed outside the town of Thirunelveli; killing 13 soldiers. Therein followed a pogrom known as "Black July,"whereby anywhere between 400 to 3,000 Tamil civilians across Colombo and other majority Sinhalese areas were massacred.

It was at such a point, that the country spiralled into a brutal 26 year long civil war that would lead to the suspected deaths of over 100,000 individuals. From jungle to coast and from village to city the war raged, leaving with it a deeply ingrained mark on a nation for many years to come.

In the rapidly dying light I pressed on out of town westerly along a narrow paved road. The climes had since dropped to allow for some reasonably innocuous cycling. The road ran parallel to a lazy paced creek and all around rice paddies glistened spectacularly. I passed a farmer of whom walked steadily alongside his water buffalo; their duties done for the day. A small group of boys splashed about in the creek as a couple of young *sari* clad girls close by loitered and giggled amongst themselves. A motorbike crept up from behind with three men on it. For a fleeting moment I was tentative. But then they soon waved at me, as one of them jovially welcomed me to Sri Lanka - before they all disappeared up ahead. The tensions of that 'Vanni incident' at such a point, were all but relieved.

The B357 north-westerly towards Pooneryn was a newly paved affair that allowed me to cruise at a leisurely 15 mph. Yet, despite gaining ground, I was soon to be engulfed in darkness. Lorries roared passed alarmingly close to my person. And despite having had my lights on, I still wondered whether or not the drivers actually saw me; or cared. It felt more like blind luck that I wasn't routinely decimated. Plus, to coincide with the dicey nights ride, I was assaulted continuously by wave upon wave of a rogue selection of kamikaze bugs; that all seemed ill-intent on slamming directly into my face. Nevertheless, to Jaffna I rode; blinded by darkness and an incalculable amount of bug juice, fuelled on eagerly by the concept of survival and much needed sleep.

I covered some 30 miles in darkness before reaching the village of Pooneryn. Just a little farther north from there was an army checkpoint that controlled access to and from Jaffna via a causeway. Several lorries had been pulled over and were being swept for anomalies. A soldier with a gun about the length of my entire body waved me down. He looked like a double hard bastard. That little lump that had appeared earlier on during the 'Vanni incident,' suddenly resurfaced in my throat.

'Hello Sir, where might you be off to this evening?' Said the soldier in some mighty fine English, as he eyed my rig over.

'Off to Jaffna Sir, if that's ok?' I said wearily.

'I see, and where might you be from?' He started flicking my gears about curiously with his thumb. Which was of course quite annoying.

'England,' I confirmed, observing the soldiers gun carelessly flapping about like a cold, steely, murderous appendage. I wondered if the safety was on. It probably was. Probably.

'Oh, very nice.' He declared as he cheekily rang my

handlebar bell.

'Err...yeah, it has its moments I guess,' partially agreeing; trying hard in no particular order not to think instinctively of rain, fog, long faces, a failed youth and BREXIT. He seemed pleased enough though, which was a good sign. Even more so when he turned the lights of my bicycle on and off and waggled his head, somewhat impressed.

'Well Sir, it's been nice to meet you,' he held out his hand and I took it. It was a solid handshake, strong and integral as one might expect from a soldier. 'Welcome to Jaffna,' he said. And the young, double hard bastard soldier motioned me through the checkpoint. For a minuscule moment in time he was all smiles, before abruptly taking on a more ascetic posture as he proceeded to wave down the next bloke on a motorbike with his big 'fuck off' gun. And as I fumbled away, my gears crunched violently like I didn't really know what the fuck I was doing - to which I guess mostly, I didn't.

10. Jaffna
யாழ்ப்பாணம் மாவட்டம்

යාපනය දිස්ත්‍රික්කය

*'There is then no sacred or profane, spiritual or sensual,
but everything that lives is pure and void.'*
- Ananda Coomaraswamy, The Dance of Śiva

Chased through the back streets of Jaffna by flea ridden pooches, from one potential guesthouse to the next, I began to think that I would never find a place to call home for the night. It was getting late, and every time my hopes were built up, the respective guesthouse owner would generally take one look at me and my rearguard of 36 army strong tail-waggers, before offering up a doleful waggle of the head. 'They're not with me!' I would utter, before another door was slammed shut in my stupid, smelly face. The mischievous canines were evidently bed-blocking me. I had to lose them somehow.

They'd all patiently sit and watch me walk to my bike, scratching a nutbag here and there or cocking a leg up against an unsuspecting neighbour. And as soon as the peddle revolutions started back up, the chase was back on. To them, it was clearly a game.

My saviour unexpectedly came in the form of the most unlikely of lilliputian heroes. Whilst tearing along a dingy, narrow alleyway aligned with high white-washed walls topped with broken fragments of glass, a short and sharp bark rang out into the depths of the night. It carried with it an air of professed authority as it echoed along the confines of the alleyway. The varying ramblings and the hot bated breath that felt mere millimetres away from tearing chunks out of my arse cheeks came to an abrupt halt. As did I. The pack were confused as to how to proceed. Something lurked in the shadows, something that disturbed them greatly. A magnificent beast stalked the night. A beast of mythical origin perhaps, with a bloodlust like no other. And then, the grand reveal. From out of the murk of a dimly lit passageway, a small but significantly predatory bundle of cutesy fluff appeared.

Holy shitballs! It's a Pomeranian, run bitches, run! The pack scarpered in all directions.

I looked down at the little feller sporting himself a proud ponytail, or in this day and age perhaps it was referred to as simply a pup-bun (I must declare that modern fashion trends and their respective namesakes often do well to evade me). Regardless, he was a handsome little chap with a fury it seemed only reserved for that of other dog-kind.

'Hey little guy,' I said. He gleefully began to wag his tail before rolling over for a belly rub. At that moment, I noted a sign on the wall, "PJ's Night Quarters." I bunglingly inched my bike through the gateway of the property and my new Pomeranian friend pottered along by my side; jumping up at my legs excitedly for more attention.

'Hello?' I called out. No answer. I propped my bicycle up against a stern looking palm tree. The front door to the property was open, and so I walked in. Behind a large reception desk an elderly gent slouched and snoozed. He donned a *kufi* cap that was about to topple. A gentle clearing of my throat however soon got his attention.

'Oh, yes sir?' As he stood, yawned and straightened his *kufi*.

'Hi, yes, I'm looking for a room please.' I replied as I dripped sweat all over the counter like an absolute slob.

'Yes sir, please follow.'

And as I followed, so did my fluffy mate. But not for long.

'Richard!' Barked the proprietor, as he motioned for the Pomeranian to go back outside. Richard??? Now, that was the icing on the cake. Of all the worldly unexpected names, Richard the Pomeranian had to be one of the most unexpected of the unexpectedly unexpected. Richie boy, the apex predator of Jaffna certainly new his place though, as he skulked off back outside to terrorise suburbia in the only way that he knew best.

My room again had a choice of three double beds to choose from, and a mildly disturbing closet bathroom that quite frankly was far too unsavoury for me to write about in this book. Therefore not quite as classy as my previous night in Vavuniya; but it would do.

'How much?' I enquired.

'How long you stay?'

'3 nights,' I confirmed.

'$6 per night,' he stated quite matter of factly.

'$5, and you got yourself a sweet deal,' I countered unreservedly.

We shook hands and waggled our heads in kind. And thus a deal was struck. A sweet deal.

After I'd washed away the days grime I chose a bed littered with the least amount of potato chip crumbs where I soon fell into a deep sleep. I dreamt of jungles littered with angry red eyes that glowed vehemently in the darkness; a place where not even the most heroic of Pomeranians dared to potter.

Jaffna City & the Islands of West Jaffna
36 miles

Prior to the civil war, Jaffna was the second most populous city in Sri Lanka. Culturally vibrant, a stronghold of Hindu-Tamil religion and culture. Historically rich, having had its own monarchy along with archeological finds that trace civilisation in the area to as far back as the Iron Age. Unfortunately, in 1981, in what some consider to be an act of ethnic biblioclasm, a band of alleged government officials and mobs for hire, raised the Jaffna library to the ground - this in response to an earlier political demonstration that had gone awry, which consequently saw the deaths of three Sinhalese police officers. The library at the time was considered to house one of the biggest collections in Asia, with over 97,000 books and palm leaf scrolls; many of which consisted of rare Tamil literature and localised historical accounts that related to the roots of Jaffna and its inhabitants.

Today, thankfully, the library has since been restored, albeit with a more modest collection of written works. The scars of conflict evident all across the city as one wanders its manic streets. The city was hit hard during the civil conflict and on three occasions changed hands between the warring factions. Gutted buildings and battered facades pop up at random. The Dutch fort, of whom's foundations were initially laid in the 1600's by the Portuguese, although succumbed to a pummelling, is today piece by piece being gradually restored through the combined efforts of the Dutch and Sri Lankan governments. For some inhabitants, the wounds may still be fresh, perhaps they always will be. But life here goes on. The town supported some new roads along with the construction of a number of retail outlets and a sparkly new shopping mall. For investment in the area is key, and as the internally displaced and those from overseas return, as does the hope of bringing further investment, so that Jaffna might someday compete on par with that of the thriving south. Thus far however, the city still had a long way to go, but unquestionably, it shows promise and integrity.

*

West of city sits a small cluster of laid back islands and islets. Some of which are joint together via recently laid causeways, whilst others need a short ferry excursion to visit. The islands are occupied by quaint villages with scenic church's and colourful temples. Farm labourers cycle to work armed with sickles and hoes, soon to attend to the flourishing rice paddies. Shrimp fisherman wade out from the causeway to Karainagar and into the shallow waters to cast, check and set their nets. A flock of diligent spoonbills stalk close by. From a classroom in Kayts, children can be heard singing harmoniously. As was now customary, a dog chased me through the streets of a small hamlet in Mandaitivu, but soon lost interest in the midday heat.

Delft was a treat, the Dutch named island is the most isolated inhabited island in Sri Lanka. Getting there requires the aid of a cramped and stinking hot ferry ride. Some 25 miles from the mainland peninsula, this charming 19 square mile car-less island trailing out into the Palk Strait hosts some of the most immaculate beaches and coral shores to be found across the country. An island of coral dry stone walls, home to wild ponies that graze freely, a 7th Century Baobab tree, a rock that grows by 2-3 mm a year, a coral fort, a deities metre long footprint and the remains of a 1000 year old stupa built during the Chola Dynasty.

Jaffna's western peninsula and its islands were dotted with a true assortment of divine gems, and at such a time I felt like one of the lucky few to be exploring its rural grace. Just as with the districts capital, the future here could be bright and full of potential, and it will be interesting to see how the area develops over the coming years. For better or for worse, one cannot truly say; for the twisted evolution of tourism has many paths.

Jaffna - Mullaitivu
89 miles

First thing saw me make an enquiry to the boss of PJ's Night Quarters as to whether I might be able to take little Richard with me on my bicycle ride. A frowning glare of a head waggle confirmed a solid no. And so, before I set off, I gave Richard, the beast of the north, one last belly rub. Jaffna was in safe paws, I was certain of it.

Dawn had only just broken like a graceful blush as I headed north-easterly out of Jaffna; like a sweaty prat on a mission. A bread van roamed the streets, making its presence known by playing jingle bells through a loudspeaker. A small herd of cows traipsed along a railway track as the low-lying sun reflected a brilliant amber glow from the steel rails beneath them. The *gopuram* of Nallur Kandaswamy Kovil, the primary shrine to the deity Lord Murugan, the Hindu god of war, also radiated proudly upon passing as a concession of topless men made their way to *pooja*.

Without question, dawn was always the most

pleasant part of the day for cycling. To witness a new day unravel in the morning calm of a new locale was always a reward. Yet, as each day progressed and flared into life and the climes began to soar with the sun rising higher into the sky, I often found that my cognitive responses began to flounder somewhat. Through a general combination of all round physical exertion, being cooked alive and sweating profusely - it took little time to succumb to a mild, if not compulsory onset of delirium. Here below, I've established a commonplace timetable for your consideration:

06:00 - 07:00 = Soothing, pleasant, life is great
07:00 - 08:00 = Charming with spicy undertones yet still happy to be an earthling
08:00 - 09:00 = The first sweat breaks, the future looks ominous
09:00 - 10:00 = Time to cook some breakfast on the asphalt
10:00 - 11:00 = I feel shapeless as a bout of mid-morning delirium begins to kick in
11:00 - 13:00 = It becomes difficult to distinguish oneself from a solid or a liquid
13:00 - 16:00 = Is this the real life? Is this just fantasy?
16:00 - 17:00 = I can just about familiarise myself with being a solid again
17:00 - 18:00 = I remember my given birth name
18:00 - 18:05 = I remember my surname

18:05 - 06:00 = Life is great again

En route to Point Pedro, amidst a discrete layer of rapidly forming spicy undertones, I stopped off at Nilavarai Well. Its turquoise waters sit squared in by a series of huge and weathered concrete blocks. It is a well of unknown depths, where legend has it that Rama once took a break. Finding himself amongst this dry and barren landscape whereby he consequently found himself in a desperate need of a thirst quencher. To solve his predicament, he fired his arrow deep into the ground to form a well of fresh and everlasting water. Like Rama, I too was thirsty, but unlike the great Hindu deity, I had come prepared and had with me a mysterious bottle of wood apple nectar that I'd picked up at a roadside convenience store. The wood apple is a fruit that if I'm honest, I'd never even heard of until visiting the shores of Sri Lanka. Yet, a fruit as common in these parts as coca is to Colombia or a pint of Stella is to a British lager lout. The juice itself looks far from appetising, looking more like colonic irrigation poop water than a healthy fruit beverage. And in hindsight, the taste perhaps wasn't too dissimilar to how it looked. Let's just say that I wasn't a fan. But in true Rama style it quenched my thirst all the same. And therefore who are we? And why are we here? If not to take the occasional culinary risk on our travels?

Farther north saw me pass through Valvettithurai, a former hotbed for smuggling and piracy and the birth town of former LTTE leader Velupillai Prabhakaran. The familiar story of bullet riddled, crumbling and untenable properties ever prevalent. Yet, the war alone was not the only factor to contribute to the regions spoliation. For on the 26th December 2004, a huge 9.2 magnitude earthquake struck off the west coast of northern Sumatra, that in turn triggered a series of tsunamis that led to the estimated deaths of over 227,898 people across 14 countries. And even though Sri Lanka lay some 1056 miles from the earthquakes epicentre, it would not be spared. The country alone saw close to 32,000 people lose their lives, with another 5,000 to 6,000 considered missing. Although the entire coastline was in someway or another affected, it was from the north of the country all the way around to the southwest that was hit the hardest; displacing close to 900,000 people. In the days to come, the carnage caused on that fateful day some 15 years before my arrival became all the more evident as I edged my way further south.

Point Pedro is Sri Lanka's northernmost point, a name stemmed from the Portuguese *"Punta das Pedras,"* meaning "The Rocky Cape." I passed a busy fish market where the smell of the days catch lingered heavy. Off the coast a collection of small colourful boats bobbed delicately upon the oceans calm azure surface. An ebullient character carrying a crateful of fish on the back of his moped slowed down next to me to say 'hi,' before thanking me for visiting his village. I told him that it was a pleasure to be there. It really was.

Having no further choice but to head south now, I picked up a small B road; the B371 to be precise. A road that runs parallel to the rambunctious A9 that would offer up a more carefree and secluded affair. And how pleasant and inoffensive a straight line can look on a map - and how deceiving they can translate to in reality. For the B371 would contain one of the toughest sections of road that I'd have to traverse in all of Sri Lanka. For close to 15 miles the road was in the process of being resurfaced and thus predominantly consisted of loose and un-compacted rock. Far from smooth for that of a motor vehicle, but simply put, pure hell for a big dummy cyclist like myself. More often than not, I had to disappointingly dismount and walk. By this point it was midday and the sun was so unrelentingly barbaric that it somehow felt illegal. The air static and shade an impossibility. The horizon before me contorted and formless, like a gaseous absurdity leaking through the Earth's surface that systematically vaporised everything in its path at a molecular level. My lips dry and cracked, took on the consistency of sandpaper. To complain was futile, the sun was my kryptonite and I was at its complete and utter mercy.

Sprawled to the right of me as I cycled along, was a vast and verdurous mangrove wetland. Out there somewhere, something guttural made itself known. The habitat was doubtlessly beautiful and the bird life exotic, but I had by such a stage fully succumbed to a classic bout of the midday delirium; and as such, very little made cognitive sense to me. A sign for land mines with a picture of a skull and crossbones scrawled across it also did little to detract me from my molten misery.

Head down, I continued with this ugly and monotonous grind. The sun customarily obliterating me with every second that passed. Until eventually, a bridge presented itself. A bridge no less that led me to the suddenly much sought after A9 - a smooth paved road that granted me sanity in the name of progress.

And as I charged south with greater gusto I soon encountered the infamous Elephant Pass. A place where once vast numbers of elephants were shepherded north into Jaffna in order to be exported over to India. A locale that was a strategically important and fiercely fought over isthmus, for it connected via a causeway the Jaffna Peninsula to the rest of mainland of Sri Lanka. A testament to the extremities of the civil war sits not so far from the northern section of the causeway. A rusting homemade tank/bulldozer devised by the LTTE. This heavily armoured and horrific looking contraption shrouded in a blend of corrugated metal, wire and spikes looked as if it had just escaped from some sort of twisted medieval futures past. It shows the ingenuity and the lengths to which the LTTE were willing to go in order to claim, hold or restore territory. And it was on the 1st July 1991, that the 'terrorist bulldozer' (as named by the Sri Lankan Army) was sent on a suicide mission to the frontline; loaded with a cornucopia of explosives and deathly horrors. Its mission however restrained at the hands of one 26 year old Corporal Gamini Kularatne, of whom was martyred when infiltrating the tank and setting off a hand grenade at close quarters.

To the opposite side of the road, atop a mound of earth just before entry to the causeway, a huge and unavoidable monument rises. Erected by the Sri Lankan Army post civil war, the monument depicts the island of Sri Lanka being raised up by a huge set of bronze hands as four equally as bronze lions sit guard upon each of its corners. Tablets at its base portray varying scenes of warfare: soldiers doing battle in the jungle, soldiers at battle in a lagoon and a naval officer and accompanying warships doing battle at sea. Whilst another more apocryphal illustration depicts the mutual shaking of hands. In all likelihood, it's questionable as to whether or not the shaking of hands part ever took place, considering how abruptly and ultra-violently the war ended (see next chapter). But, it is this concept of a peace without the foray of death that should be heeded. For long may that peace reign on the teardrop island.

8. Mullaitivu**
முல்லைத்தீவு மாவட்டம்
මුලතිවු දිස්ත්‍රික්කය

'When you are shopping for a cow, make sure that the price of the tail is included.' - Tamil proverb

My burned and tired body laboured on towards the coastal town of Mullaitivu. The SPF 50 sunscreen that I had purchased from a small convenience store back in Jaffna had turned out to be either out of date, or just fake. The skin upon my face, neck, forearms and legs beamed an embarrassing shade of lobster red. The pain forthwith spoke of a restless nights sleep. Yet, sleepless nights were certainly no oddity along this coast of somnolent fishing settlements; haunted not only by that of the trauma of the 2004 Boxing Day tsunami, but the bitter end of the country's blood soaked civil war. After the fall of the Jaffna Peninsula to the SLA, the remaining LTTE retreated to the jungles and surrounds of Mullaitivu - this was to be the guerrillas last stand and for thousands of innocents, their final hours. Corralled into a small slither of land and an apparent no fire zone, civilians mixed in with combatants, were bombarded by the artillery heavy SLA - leading to one of the largest humanitarian disasters in living history. By the 18th May 2009, the nearly 26 year long civil war that had began on the 23rd July 1983, was officially declared over. By the time LTTE chief of command Vellupillai

Prabakharan and his high ranking cadres were found dead at Nandikadal lagoon, over 100,000 people had lost their lives.

A strong wind puckered up and carried inland off the ocean, somewhat soothing my burns. And yet, in the grand scheme of things, my dismal pain really wasn't anything. Mullaitivu, with all of its struggles, like so many a hard hit settlements that I had journeyed to and from throughout the north, had just kept going. The will of humanity strong; through hardships unimaginable it strives to succeed. To embellish what is now, and to hone the reins to the ideal of a less fragmented future. This was pivotal, for the sake of everyone.

Among a fading light I cycled along a freshly paved road that led towards the ocean. The streets were aligned with a combination of rubble clustered plots and new builds; one of which was the suitably named 'The Big House.' This immaculate looking high walled compound sat mere metres from the coast, where an all smiling chubby fellow greeted me; before leading me through a to a small courtyard where I parked up my bicycle for the night.

In the doorway to the property stood and elderly *sari* clad lady, her eyes denoted wisdom.

'Welcome Mr Daniel,' she said. *Wow! She knows my name!* I thought, before I countered my well earned dimness with the memory that I had in fact made the reservation online just shortly before leaving Jaffna early that very morning.

The lady ushered me inside. 'Your face so very red,' she commented.

'Look like, so much alien boy,' added the chubby fellow, quite jovially in fact as he closed the door behind me.

'Wow! Alien boy, you charmer, cheers matey.' I quipped.

He chuckled and his heavy set moustache seemed to tag along for the ride as it jerked up and down mechanically as if operated by that of an invisible puppeteer. And as he showed me to my clean, second floor room I caught the first glimpses of my face in a mirror. It turned out that my host wasn't far off the mark with his comments. For I did indeed look like a stranger from a distant planet; one trying his best to blend in with society with his embarrassingly deep fried and crispy red face mask that he'd quite clearly purchased from an intergalactic conman.

'Ow,' I soliloquised. I instinctively looked away in disgust, cowering like an exposed monstrosity. It was true, I was hideous, but more urgently, I was dirty and tired. Hideosity would have to wait.

I took a delicately cold shower, which offered up an element of rejuvenation, as it soothed my throbbing burns. My hair was as as stiff as a builder's yard brush and the skin on my legs layered with an ochre taint. Dirt and grit rinsed from my being and collected like bedrock on the tile floor.

Outside, dusk had already been stripped and painted in darkness by the colour of night. From my bedroom window I could see St. Peter's tsunami memorial church. A low-light emanated from somewhere within as the moonlight reflected off of the church's crucifix and cast its name across the night sky. I laid back atop my bedsheets; it being too warm to sink beneath them. The wind brought the sound of the ocean to the very foundations of The Big House. And as I closed my eyes, the waters felt ever closer; lapping all so gently at the shores of my room, an inducingly rhythmic and tranquillising calm; Natures lullaby would soon send me on my way.

Mullaitivu - Trincomalee
57 miles

A bread van passed The Big House at 05:30am, blaring out the theme tune to the Phantom of the Opera. I supposed it was time to get up anyway.

Downstairs, my hosts prepared me a breakfast of lukewarm coffee, accompanied by watery eggs and a stack of microwaved bread. They watched me as I ate, making sure everything was in order. As a whole it wasn't, but I gave the impression that it was anyway. I'm very low maintenance like that. Give me a plate of stir-fired macaque muck and I'll try my very best to pass it off as a perfectly acceptably staple cuisine; just as long as everyone gets to keep face. Plus, no one likes a whinger. I gave a two thumbs fresh salute after I'd finished up, and my hosts all seemed delighted; especially my hosts moustache, of which flexed away contentedly to itself long after even its owner had seemingly done away with his smiley proceedings. I'd miss that tash; such flair, such...panache.

Before setting off for the day, my mornings risk assessment would largely be focused around not attaining sunburn upon my sunburns; therefore I'd cover up my still vibrant coloured skin with a snood and a long sleeved shirt. I'd sweat well, but it would be a necessity under the circumstances. The hope was to find genuine sunscreen at my days goal of Trincomalee.

After some quick maintenance checks, I slipped onto a coastal road and out of town. The ocean looked as it so often did - beautiful and lonely. The air, tight and the firmament, pasty; as if somehow offended.

I gradually flanked inland somewhat and for a while traversed a neat yet quiet and unassuming road that eventually merged to dirt. I bobbed along with an element of uncertainty as the track gradually narrowed. After a short time, a tightly packed and makeshift cluster of corrugated dwellings materialised. Roofs were held down with tyres and bricks and walls propped up by palms. At first, through the litter strewn streets where smoke lingered, little seemed to stir. An electricity pylon fizzed worryingly overhead. A decrepit rickshaw jacked up on its side, minus a tyre with no place to go. A line of empty plastic chairs sat under a veranda, amongst a carpet of spent cigarettes and empty beer bottles. And from somewhere, a cockerel staked its territorial claim. The quiet morning amble was soon jilted though - as from a series of discreet passageways a profusion of children suddenly emerged. They chased me with their hands out as I cycled along - 'moneeeey,' they cried excitedly. They obviously knew something that I didn't.

Before long, I'd hit the end of the road, where I'd come face to face with a vast body of water: Kokkilai lagoon. This near 12 square mile body of brackish water not only marks the end of the line, but also distinguishes both district borders of Mullaitivu and Trincomalee, along with that of the Northern and Eastern Provinces. A very fluid border in every sense of the word. One that could well be deemed a challenge to one self-proclaimed man and his bicycle; our all round general buoyancy was certainly up for debate.

As I'd come to such an abrupt stop, the pursuing children had by this stage caught up with me; their hands held out expectantly. I feigned emptying my pockets to reveal nothing but emptiness. They were having none of it as they mischievously pointed to my handlebar pannier where it was safe to say that I kept a small stash of greenery. To grease the palms of expectancy however didn't feel like the right move. Therefore I kept up the slapstick act of pretending not to see what it was that they were pointing at. Close by, a fisherman with a Chelsea F.C baseball cap squatted upon the bow of a small motorboat; a cigarette hung carelessly from his lips. Amongst the commotion I noticed a glimmer of a smirk as he leapt from his vessel and onto the muddy shores of the lagoon. He clapped his hands on the approach and shouted something abusive sounding at the children. In an instant they were running away and giggling amongst themselves.

The fisherman said something to me that I didn't understand; but I assumed he was offering me a lift across the lagoon. I pointed at myself and my bike and then gestured to the other side to clarify. He waggled his head in acknowledgment, before grabbing a stick and writing a number in the dirt: "1500." I suddenly saw why these children saw me as such a disposable source of wealth. 1,500 Rs seemed a little steep. Not that I was any expert in South Asian lagoon crossing tariffs. I felt however that I was obliged and expected to barter. But if there was one thing I hated doing in this world, apart from changing the duvet cover or eating quiche - it was bartering. I asked to borrow the fisherman's stick, to which he happily lent me for free. I crossed out the "1" to leave "500," by all means still a tad excessive but a lesser bullet to take all the same. The fisherman simpered at my bartering inadequacies as he reclaimed the stick of destiny. He returned the "1" to the figure: "1500." He wasn't budging one iota. I exclaimed to the good sir that the price seemed marginally ridiculous. The fisherman haughtily shrugged his shoulders and pointed at the price again. The only way around the lagoon across dry land involved some serious backtracking to the tune of some 40 miles. He had my metaphoric gonads in a vice; grinding them with indifference. I nodded my head in both defeat and disgust as I pulled out my cash to discover that I only had two 1000 Rs notes. I saw the fisherman's glow, he knew what was coming.

'Erm....change?' I asked rather meekly, already knowing the answer. He waggled his head in what I took to be a very obvious 'no.' For a parsimonious man such as myself, this was a bitter pill to swallow, but felt that I had little choice as I begrudgingly handed over 2000 rupees of cold hard cash. The fisherman's eyes shone majestically, like two well polished carnelian gemstones. I'd been ripped a new one, and not for the first time on my travels, I'd soon look like a knackered old mechanics rag. However, if I could afford to be in Sri Lanka doing what I was doing, I could afford a financial predicament, or eight. And thus, my bartering skills were officially declared utter shite.

The fisherman helped me load my bike and panniers precariously onto the swaying boat as I clumsily clambered aboard. I perched myself on the gunwale and the fisherman handed me a lit cigarette. I didn't smoke, but somehow right there at that very moment it didn't seem to matter. From the transom the fisherman pulled the starter chord and the boats engine spluttered hesitantly into life. We were soon chugging across the murky lagoon. I took a drag on my cigarette as I thought about the 2000 rupees that I'd never see again. So this was what the price of indignity tasted like.

11. Trincomalee
திருகோணமலை
ත්‍රිකුණාමලය

'A cow eats moving, a house eats standing.'
- Tamil proverb

The crossing shorter than I expected as I was dumped on a rogue spit of sand that acted as a barrier, separating ocean from lagoon. 'Bye, bye Mr Red Face,' declared the fisherman, before he fired his boat back up and departed back to Kokkilai. Cheeky git, so, he could speak English after all. I laughed it off in haphazard disgust as I positioned my panniers back upon their respective racks. I took a glug of water from my once again nearly exhausted canteen. This effort alone enough to make me sweat to the point that I was beginning to wonder if I might actually have hyperhidrosis…of the face. Well, anyhoo, I'd just have to worry about that later, it was time to make tracks (literally!). For the sand was far too thick to cycle through, forcing me to drag it across the spit; gorging a deep scar in the sand with my wheels as I teetered along at a snails pace. Midday had since breached as rivulets of perspiration continued to pour off my being. I drank more water - as sparingly as ever. After some time, I closed in upon a small dock on the other side of the lagoon where a small path emerged that would soon guide me on my way to Trincomalee.

For great stretches the roads were being used to dry freshly harvested rice. I felt certain that under the baking heat, that it surely wouldn't take long. Young boys kept guard and waved sticks at any overly curious crows. Farther along, a pack of langur monkeys swaggered across the road and into the scrub; their long tails whipped about vivaciously above the vegetation line, like fluffy equivalents of H.R Giger's Aliens.

As I encroached upon the outskirts of Trincomalee, the pace of life picked up. Along a narrow lane that swung towards the beach a row of guesthouses, coffee shops, restaurants and juice bars stretched. Sun scorched white men walked topless down the street, whilst a couple of girls with a mediterranean flair about them strutted confidently along in skimpy bikinis with rolled up yoga mats under their arms. I'd found myself an east coast tourist hub.

Where as the previous night in Mullaitivu I'd spent it at 'The Big House,' in Trincomalee I based myself at the rather eloquent 'The Little House.' A quaint white walled bungalow set amongst a charming and well loved garden that offered up some much sought after shade. There was also a hammock salaciously poised between a couple of palms for that all important mid-afternoon siesta. I was checked in hastily by Szymek, the kindly Polish manager, before heading back out into the garden to pay a visit to the all too enticing hammock. For a siesta was most certainly in order.

* * *

Trincomalee
9 miles

I took an early morning stroll down to Uppuveli Beach. It was a mostly deserted affair, a few beach dogs lounged around or fought one another playfully in the sand, whilst an aged man wandered carefree along the threshold of the tideline, hands clasped behind his back. These in a way were luxuries not always afforded at this time of year. For Sri Lanka has a complex weather system - having two monsoon seasons affecting two different parts of the island at separate times of the year. From May to September, the south-west of the country gets battered by what is known locally as the *yala* season. And then, from October to February, the slightly less formidable *maha* season interrogates the north and east of the island. Now at the back end of January, hotels still lay largely desolate, the beaches vacant, the sands far from pristine and the oceans waters choppy and uninviting. In little over a months time this would all change. But for now, these eastern shores lay melodramatically deserted.

For breakfast, I had some fresh fruit from one of the few quaint guest houses to offer up a menu to out of season tourists. Incidentally, most of the other foreign faces that I had seen on my short ride into town yesterday were also present. For the most part we all politely ignored one another, apart from a Swiss games developer of whom approached me to ask if I could play his mobile video game that he had been working on for the past 18 months. I did, and it was pure button bashing dross. Yet, I told him it was very engaging and that I best return his phone to him incase I should get too addicted. He seemed pleased with my falseness. I didn't have the heart to tell him the truth of the matter, through risk of ruinomg the poor fellows holiday/or life. From first hand experience, I know only too well how much it pains one to be told that after years of dedicated graft that your passion project sucks arse. The brutalness of strangers was a reality, an ever-given, a right 'ol fucker.

I took a short ride into town after breakfast. Its composure was far flung from that of the barren shores of Uppuveli. A manic ambience greeted me as a mishmash of shops competed for custom. A one way traffic system recognised and seemingly obeyed, plus a miniature roundabout with a white and red clock tower marooned at its centre.

Farther south of town and the traffic petered away. Inland a herd of deer grazed upon an unkempt cricket pitch, whilst by the coast, the beach lay littered with small fishing rigs that would do well to survive the presently rough monsoonal waters. Cutting inland from here, was the world's fifth largest natural harbour. Due to its shape it was known locally in sanskrit as *Gokarna*, meaning 'cow's ear.' An area throughout history of geographic significance for both economic and militaristic means. Just to the north of the harbour sits

Fort Frederik, a coat of arms emblazoned across the top of a stone archway; it reads *'dieu et mon droit.'* The British being the last of the colonial powers in Sri Lanka to leave their stamp. The fort however dates back to 1623, when the Portuguese ransacked potentially 4th Century BCE Koneswaram Kovil - atop Swami Rock, sometime in 1622. Many a riches were plundered, and much lost to the surrounding sea whilst the ruins of the temple were used in the construction of the Fort of Triquillimale, that would later be named Fort Frederik by the Portuguese's successors: the Dutch. Centuries later, and an underwater archaeology expedition led by none other than science fiction writer Arthur C. Clarke, would recover an abundance of once thought lost sculptures and relics. This recovery led to an incentive in the 1950's to return Koneswaram Kovil to its former glory at the summit of Swami Rock.

As I breached the stonewall of the fort, I found myself amongst the presence of the Sri Lankan Army. A number of buildings and barracks lay shaded amongst a cluster of mature trees. A steep path, that of the ancient pilgrim's - soon ascended. An almost instantaneous sheen of sweat gathered upon my forehead as a prickly sensation coaxed my spine and the back of my shirt became saturated. The gradient was a truly testing one, yet I was thankful that my bicycle wasn't fully laden and that I only had to conquer some 350 ft,. Otherwise, I had no doubts about busting out a hernia.

I came to a halt at a sign that said 'No Shoes.' Close

by, a small booth was situated for the depositing of one's footwear. I locked my bike to a railing and proceeded to the booth. I short man with a grey and well defined pencil drawn moustache appeared on the other side of the booth to collect my trainers. I felt abjectly bad for him, for every second that he would get to spend with that hideous pair of stinkers. It was a smell that had evolved beyond reasonable doubt into something quite ghastly. A smell that inspired bacterial infection. A smell, that wholeheartedly, I wouldn't wish upon my worst enemy; fetid, with a hint of evil incarnate. And as I handed them over, there was no courteous head waggle in return, merely an unabashed nose waggle of truth and a wince trapped somewhere between disdain and disgust. The poor fellow would struggle to sleep that night and his well defined moustache would assuredly wilt. Thusly, I apologised unreservedly for that knowing fact.

On the approach to the apex of Swami Rock, a huge weather beaten statue of Shiva met me. Koneswaram, meaning 'Lord of the Sacred Hill,' is dedicated chiefly to Lord Shiva and is the easternmost shrine of the five Iswarams in Sri Lanka. It is said that here, Indra, King of the Gods, worshipped alongside Ravana - the Demon King of Lanka...and his mum.

I entered the *kovil*, where devotees paid their respects to deities at varying shrines, altars and paintings. There was a calm within; respectful and welcoming. When the Portuguese first set foot here they marvelled at the temple complex that lay before them. The catholic priest Fernão de Quieroz, labelled it 'Rome of the Pagans of the Orient.' And then, his colleagues systematically raised the temple complex to the ground in a brutish act of religious zealotism.

Upon exiting the *kovil*, I faced east and marvelled at the grandiose blue carpet of the Bay of Bengal. At 839,000 square miles, it is the largest body of water to be called a bay in the world. Here, the rivers of India, Bangladesh, Myanmar, Indonesia and of course Sri Lanka all contribute. Many a great adventurers, traders, interlopers and missionaries had crossed this expanse: Ibn Battuta, William Dampier, Thomas Pitt, Adoniram Judson. Some lived, some perished. Alas, the Bay of Bengal was no place for a bloke and his bike. I was a minuscule adventurer in the grand scheme of things, and a proud landlubber at that. For my fate now lay upon the long (ideally dry) road back to Colombo.

12. Anuradhapura
අනුරාධපුර දිස්ත්‍රික්කය
அனுராதபுரம் மாவட்டம்

'Having curry for breakfast is a thing of beauty.'
 - Romesh Ranganathan

Trincomalee - Anuradhapura
61 miles

As to oust any correlation to me being deemed a linear cyclist, I today changed my directive and headed westerly inland, towards the ancient capital of Anuradhapura. I bundled along the little frequented A12 whilst the sun traditionally raged over my shoulder; a mere 20 yards away. Such as tradition, the onset delirium wasn't too far from taking hold.

For brunch, I stopped by at a little eatery on the outskirts of Kahatagasdigiliya. It was a vague looking building, in fact if it wasn't for the overwhelmingly beautiful stench of curry flirting with my nasal passages I could quite easily have cycled past what many might've considered as merely a hole in a wall. For essentially, that was all it was. I propped my bicycle up against an honest looking block or mortar and let my nose guide me forth. Seconds later and a low thud ensued; I didn't even need to turn to see what had happened, for it was an all too familiar trend when on the road. My bike had just power-slammed itself into the dirt in some sort of act of velocipedic rebellion, a bit like that out of control brat in Sainsbury's that collapses in a heap on aisle 4 because mother downright refuses him a carton of Um Bongo. Tantrums are best avoided, therefore I decided to pay the stubborn heap of well crafted alloy no heed and ventured into the hole in the wall.

Inside it was a small barebones room of limited aesthetics, whereby the menu evidently appeared to be splashed liberally across its potentially once beige interior. An elderly lady fanned herself behind a counter with a few select metal trays of curry, daal and sambal poised before her; each of which looked equally as volatile and ever slightly more intimidating than the other. But that was fine, for my mind was open, as my stomach was empty. The lady eyed me wearily as if I might be trouble, she wasn't to be the first lady to eye me in such a way, and doubtlessly wouldn't be the last. I neutralised the situation by rubbing my belly progressively, before pointing to a yellowly-green dish of potential malcontent. The lady soon waggled her head in approval and gestured for me to have a seat. And no sooner had I seated did I find myself surrounded by an assortment of dishes and rotis as a feast fit for a Vanniyar was presented before me. The elderly lady gestured for me to tuck in as she farted and tottered off back to the kitchen. A fart I figured to be logical and well placed in the grand scheme of things;

for if you're going to guff anywhere, it may just as well be in a curry house amongst all the other extravagant aromas kicking about. Yet most importantly, she owned the moment and therefore that was something to be proud of. I know I was.

Guff-gags aside, it also hadn't taken me too long to gain an audience as a number of locals came to watch me enjoy my fiery feast. They smiled and nodded at me, motioning for me to eat more. That of course, as a calorie burning cyclist I committed to as a matter of diligent purpose as I went on to consume probably my own body weight in lava infused curry. Some might find having an audience watch you push food into your fat-face somewhat off-putting, yet these were merely esoteric curiosities that come part and parcel of being a minority. My Sri Lankan audience however soon lost interest in me, or were decisively grossed out by my lavish appetite and rigorous amounts of sweating, as they soon thinned out and took their respective leave.

Back outside, I felt like I'd just eaten a hand grenade. I picked up my aluminium brat and dusted it down, before prepping myself for another blazing afternoon in the saddle.

Farther along the A12 and the dry zone that I currently found myself in became less apparent. From a distance, a thirsty and weary traveller could very well mistake one for a mirage in this dry and seemingly unforgiving landscape. Yet, gather a little closer, and the mirage is evidently a reality and one of the masterstrokes of the ancient Sinhalese world. For an oasis lay before me; with its waters that sparkled and lay clustered with thick rafts of lily pads. A vibrant array of dragonflies patrolled erratically. Nearby, children swung from a piece of rope that dangled precariously from a sturdy overhanging tree branch, before they splashed down into the cool relief below. In an area that sees less than 75 inches of rainfall over the course of a 3 month period, water becomes one the most valuable, if not the most priceless of commodities to the existence of life. The ancients of the country copped onto this nearly two millennia ago and thus devised *wevas*, often referred to as tanks; essentially an irrigation system whereby huge connecting bunds act as a reservoir to encapsulate water for surrounding communities. Dotted across some 15,000 square miles of traditionally dry land, there are today about 30,000 such tanks still proudly conserving water, each one echoing a marvel of ancient engineering.

I would pass several such tanks en route to Anuradhapura, before coming to a stop at Nuwara Wewa - the largest tank in the city. With a bund that stretches 3 miles long it is capable of holding some 1500 million cubic feet of water. Evening wasn't far off, as I wheeled my bike up the side of its steep embankment, where in the shade of a colossal tree that had had the centre of it completely bored out, I took a seat and peered out across the lake. Its waters still a shade of auburn as the sun sunk low in the sky. On the opposite side of the bank, rising up above the tree line, a blend of communications masts and stupas stood firm; a merger of new and old worlds that slowly turned to shadow. And then, with nothing but blood and misery in mind, the local mosquito populace of Anuradhapura sought me out. It was time to find some digs.

Anuradhapura - Mihintale - Anuradhapura
20 miles

For my time spent in Anuradhapura I sought out the Fig & Gecko Hostel. A charming whitewashed 1930's colonial house set within the shady confines of a tree clustered garden. It offered up a much welcome break from the severity of the sweltering daytime climes. The hostel also works in conjunction with Give a Fig, an NGO that offers volunteering opportunities whilst supporting the local community. Paul, a north-Londoner and one of the kindly and enthusiastic members of management was a wealth of local knowledge, and before I set out for the day suggested a particular route to undertake in which to explore and get the most out of my time in this historical city.

The first established Kingdom of Sri Lanka and one of the longest continuously inhabited cities in the world, Anuradhapura was founded in 377 BC by King Pandukabhaya. It was the centrifugal point for Theravada Buddhism within the country, that in turn influenced its people: the Sinhalese. And therefore, guided the architecture of the city with a vast and awe inspiring collection of buildings that incorporated stupas, monasteries and pokunas of all varying shapes and sizes; from the modest to the grandiose.

From the outskirts, to the east of the city, there was no questioning in which direction one should be headed. Rising high above the lush rice paddies, like a weather beaten pumpkin wearing a mortarboard, stands Jetavanaramaya. When erected by King Mahasena sometime between 273-301 AD, the structure stood at a staggering 122 metres; making it at the time, the world's tallest stupa. And, after the pyramids of Egypt, the third tallest structure in the ancient world. Its original incarnation was however destroyed in raids by the armies of South India. But today, still stands at a respectable 71 metres and has of course long been outstripped by the skyscrapers of the 20th and 21st Centuries. However, with a base area of 2,508,000 square feet (about 3 football pitches) and roughly 93.3 million bricks (a shit load of Lego), the grand old stupa can still claim to be the largest stupa of its kind - in the world. In its presence, I felt ant-like and inferior. To even touch it felt like a crime, as the sun seemed to scorn me as I gazed up at the giant stupas broken pinnacle.

I cycled on leisurely around the city, noticing a sudden influx of tourists that I hadn't otherwise witnessed so much during my travels throughout the north. *There's one,* I noted to myself as I spotted a rotund chap in ridiculously short, shorts waddle penguin-esque along the pavement. He seemed to stop momentarily on my passing to mop a gallon of sweat from his forehead with his elbow, before going on to curse the climes in traditional Texan - 'Goddammit, it's hotter than the devils asshole up in here!'

Oh look, there's another one! A tall woman this time, with short blonde cropped hair. She was harvesting a Cornetto whilst making damn well sure that she got at least 87,012 selfies of the momentous occasion to share with false online friends that mostly wouldn't give a fuck about her exploits.

The spectacle of other foreigners bar myself naturally not quite outweighing the sheer magnificence of the works of the ancients of course, but, in some small way, made me feel slightly more chameleon like during my touristic endeavours.

I purchased a Cornetto and took a selfie before straying westerly.

Soon thereafter, another striking hemispherical stupa lured me in. Ruwanwelisaya, with a circumference of 370 feet and a height of 180 feet, it is the third largest stupa in Sri Lanka - pure white with a gold tipped pinnacle, it gleamed fantastically under the furnace of the sun. The tiles around the complex absorbed the dwarf stars rays passionately and burned the bare soles of my feet. Many other a curious tourists could also be seen tiptoeing across what must have been the nearest equivalent to hot coals as they all desperately sought the cover of shade. A form of penance no doubt whilst in the presence of such grandness. For historically, Anuradhapura is a truly captivating city to explore, one to fully submerge the imagination. The ancient Sinhalese are to be applauded for such fine works and craftsmanship.

Further escapades took me to the rock temple of Isurumuiya Vihara, the first century ruins of Ratna Prasada and to Mahamewna Park - home to Thuparamaya, the oldest dagoba in the country, dating back to well over 200 BC. It was here also that the oldest living human-planted tree in the world can be found; and a fig tree at that. The Sri Maha Bodhi Tree was brought to Sri Lanka as a sapling in 236 BC by Sanghamitta, the daughter of India's King Asoka. It would later be planted in its present day locale by King Devanampiya Tissa in 288 BC. The sapling is said to come directly from the exact same Bodhi Tree that the Buddha attained enlightenment under, thus making it sacred to all Buddhists. Protected by a golden fence with its larger branches supported by joists of gold, many a pilgrims and devotees were gathered at the base of the tree, where they offered prayer and committed to mantras. A survivor of storms and acts of terrorism; it is a truly venerated fig tree.

It was towards mid-afternoon, just about when the heat had began to drain a vast quantity of my life-forces out of me, that I headed back to the accommodating shade of the garden at the Fig & Gecko. The plan was to have a siesta of sorts, perhaps catch up on some reading. But after chatting to Paul, of whom was now sporting himself a dashing *kurta* and in the midsts of prising a gecko out of the jaws of an overly curious puppy, he was having none of it. He firmly insisted that I take a trip to Mihintale, 10 miles east of town, for it wielded a sundown that would be unforgivable to miss. Not one to shy away from the occasional sunset, I fetched my wheels.

Mihintale is the purported cradle of Buddhism in Sri Lanka. In the 3rd Century BC, Mahinda, the Buddhist missionary and Arahat son of India's King Ashoka, came to Sri Lanka to preach the Buddhist doctrine. It was atop Aradhana Gala, a distinctly awkward looking boulder stacked some 300 metres upon the summit of the plateau of Mihintale, that Mahinda first preached to King Devanampiyatissa. So hooked upon the concept and ideals of Buddhism was the King, that he promptly declared it the country's official religion. It would soon gain momentum across the island, where present day it still remains as the most followed religion in the country - some 70% of the islands population.

Many pilgrims flock to Mihintale, especially during the full moon of June, which is said to have been the time when Mahinda first met the King. It was now however late January, and apart from myself and a French couple mounting an ascent upon the 1,840 granite steps to the summit, there were very few other visitors.

Since its conception as a sacred site, Mihintale became a hermitage for Buddhist monks, with a number of cave dwellings that lay spread across its range. Signs ask visitors to be respectful and to allow the monks to meditate in peace. A gobby group of macaques subordinately refused to follow suit as they fought and hollered amongst themselves up in the frangipani trees. They, along with the French, were however a minority around these parts. '*Merde, il fait chaud!*' I overheard, as I double-stepped past a sweat sodden and sizeable octogenarian of a man, of whom clearly had no idea beforehand to what his wife had signed him up for. He was quite clearly having a holiday the very opposite to that of the cool and airy vineyards of Beaujolais. Up ahead of him, a much slimmer and altogether more healthier looking individual of whom I took to be the Monsieur's wife. She soon turned to usher on her spouse with some words of encouragement: '*dépêchez-vous gros homme.*'

'*Cette femme sera la mort de moi,*' declared the tubby husband, in a seething if not slightly petulant tone. All the while his face a periodic table of sheer pain and misery.

At the summit, the Maha Seya Stupa beamed proudly; an annual lick of white paint more than seeing to this. Inside, the Urna Roma Dhathuwa, the sacred white hair relic of the Buddha. From there and barely a stone's throw away now, was the Aradhana Gala, aka 'Meditation Rock,' or dependent upon one's source, the

'Rock of Invitation.' It was here that the great monk Mahinda, delivered his aforementioned sermon. At the rocks base, a steel railing guides visitors and pilgrims up a collection of some precariously steep steps cut directly into the rock. Some might consider the pathway a health and safety inspectors nightmare; especially on a windy and cursed day. But in the name of devotion, come rain or shine, pilgrims have a path to follow, and therefore they shall always prevail - unless of course they perish.

As light began to fail me, I scaled to the boulders summit. From somewhere down below a Frenchman cursed and threatened something about a divorce settlement. Atop, the view bore down upon a sweeping landscape of assorted and rapidly darkening greens that filtered into a hazy horizon; smeared oppressively by the dying embers of day. Bats freshly arisen from their slumber began to swarm the dusk skies as little black flecks dotted the field of view; making the sight seem like I was watching a knackered and overplayed reel of one of Mother Nature's finest movies.

The freedom that elated me at that exact moment was pure, the beauty of it carved pricelessly to memory. I'd need not notes, nor pictures, merely the will to exist and the mind to reminiscence. And even though the cycle ride back to Anuradhapura in the dark was to prove haphazard with a hint of mental, it was worth it. Everything right then, through risk and uncertainty was more than worth it. 'Happy Days,' as they say.

13. Matale
මාතලේ දිස්ත්‍රික්කය
மாத்தளை மாவட்டம்

'When the dogs bark at the moon, the moon is not brought down because of it.' - Sinhalese proverb

Anuradhapura - Dambulla
41 miles

The air was static, everything seemed to either bake, fry, sizzle or melt. The suns rays pounded the earths surface like a Death Stars turbo-laser. Shade, became a rare, yet valuable commodity. On the outskirts of Anuradhapura, I trailed along a dirt track that curtailed a large tank; a momentary detour from the monotonous drone of the A9 south to Dambulla. For a while, a tranquil peace honed the surrounds. A hoopoe probed the dry earth of the tanks bund; its vibrant and speckled crown slicked back like an avian fashion statement. Amongst the shallow periphery of the tank's waters a woman did her laundry. Whilst farther along a lone buffalo lolled in the shallows; its leathery skin with the look of a well sheened carapace. He flapped his big ears and snorted in luxury as I passed. At that moment, I was certain that he was the most content water buffalo in all of South Asia.

The path soon led onto the rambunctious A9 that saw

me on my way to downtown Dambulla. There, I bounced and cursed my way along a road of unnatural vulgarity. A vegetable wholesalers, the biggest in all of Sri Lanka, was a troublesome encounter whereby legions of trucks that overflowed with produce competed with me for tightly contested road space. A stray watermelon that lingered by the roadside was made an example of by some 30 odd tonne metal behemoth - exploding on contact in a melodramatic fashion that only really a watermelon could get away with. As is the norm here, the general rule of thumb is that a cyclist has no right of way, just the right to die, should he/she/they - not respect that said rule of thumb. A fancy white Lexus passed me, and from its open window an Australian accented stranger commented, - 'you're pretty brave mate!' *Or, just pretty fucking stupid*, I thought.

I continued to muscle my way through the hubbub until arriving at the inquisitively named Oasis Welfare Centre - my accommodation for the next couple of nights. Down a narrow and dusty path lay a basic seaweed coloured bungalow; ramshackle yet cutesy. Just outside the property an armed man greeted me. It had appeared that I'd arrived amidst a turf war between man and simian. A pack of monkeys with shockingly terrible hairstyles that looked like they were off to a 90's rave with Danny Dyer, worked their way across the bungalows corrugated rooftop whilst a slingshot wielding man systematically fired rocks in their general direction. One of the monkeys was a huge and fearsome looking bastard, with an opaque eye and a big scar across his face like some kind of Disney villain. He appeared to curse back in simian, no doubt something about him having his sweet revenge upon mankind. He bared his gnashers before disappearing up into the tree canopy; his brethren partygoers following not far behind.

'Monkey bad,' proclaimed the man with the slingshot, before gesturing me towards the bungalow. I parked my bike up and entered the abode.

Inside, a pack of well groomed dogs lay in an idle heap; completely nonplussed by my entrance. One of them half opened a dreary eye, yet just for a curious moment, before licking her lips and returning to her siesta. In the middle of the living space a young latino woman sat splayed in hot pants and a skimpy white tank-top; leaving very little left for the imagination. Legend has it, that this was yoga. On a door to the side of the living space by a sleeping tom cat with half an ear, slingshot man pointed to my room. As he did this, a coalition of footsteps impacted across the corrugated rooftops above and amplified throughout the dwelling. One of the dogs growled in his slumber as slingshot man instinctively loaded up and headed back out into the warzone, leaving me to my own devices.

My room was small, more of a cell really, and the air within of a recycled quality. But, more than perfectly habitable for a roving vagabond such as myself. Plus, I only had to sleep in it. I dumped my gear and headed back out.

The Welfare Centre itself was poised perfectly for Dambulla's big draw: the Dambulla cave temple. Situated some 350ft up in the hills, above a huge golden statue of Buddha, lay five caves that act as dedicated shrine rooms. Across the complex there are some 150 odd statues of Buddha and 2,100 square metres of minutely detailed mural paintings dedicated to his life. These delicately lit caves of varying sizes stem back to sometime during the 3rd century BC. The temple itself, along with its statues and paintings arose later, around the 1st century BC. It was here, that King Valagamba, the exiled king of Anuradhapura, spent some 14 years living under the protection and secrecy of the local monks. As a mark of gratitude to these monks, when the King was returned to his throne, he established the cave temple; where for the past 22 centuries it has become a sacred pilgrimage site for countless numbers.

After an hour or so of mooching around the caves I ventured back down the hill. Upon the descent I purchased a wad of juicy looking mango slices from a hawker. A fundamentally regrettable faux pas. One that sore me appreciate slingshot mans born hatred of all things monkey business. They came from nowhere, their groping and mischievous hands of ill repent. The flashback imagery of their scandalous centre partings still haunt me to this very day. A collection of bickering screams from both man and monkey echoed out across

the hills, before I suddenly found myself completely
denuded of mango slices. Even that one solitary slice
that I'd just popped into the orifice of my mouth mere
milliseconds before had been swiftly vacated by some
slick and wise monkey fingers as I lay ruffled in a heap
close to the base of the hill; sweaty and tormented. And
just to make sure that my dignity was in utter tatters,
some Buddhist monk children that happened to be
passing at the time, took it upon themselves to point
and laugh at my misfortune. I had just experienced
sheer monkey tomfoolery of the worst proportion, and
for that, Buddhism was laughing at my expense. I
found this to be most unchristian like. Deep down, my
sense's told me that scarface had somehow
masterminded this atrocity, and that he had after all
exacted his sweet, sweet vengeance. I hastily retreated
back to my digs where an enquiry into the price of a
slingshot was in order.

Dambulla - Sigiriya - Dambulla
28 miles

Tree branches jutted up out of the waters of Lake
Kandalama, like twisted fingers reaching up from the
underworld. It was a pleasant and largely remote
morning of cycling around lakes, past paddies and
through some small clumps of jungle. On a route that
would eventually see me loop back on myself before
returning to the Welfare centre in Dambulla.

Yet not before calling in upon the UNESCO World Heritage site of Sigiriya, aka Lion Rock. One of the most heavily visited sites in the country and locally coined Eighth Wonder of the World. A colossal lump of rock formed from the magma of a long extinct volcano. With sheer vertical sides it elevates to 200 metres as an all captivating anomaly amongst a largely low-lying landscape of lush jungle bloom. In the 5th century, King Kashyapa declared it his capital and had a citadel built upon the rocks plateau summit. The site became his strategic bastion in order to keep an eye out for his vengeful brother Moggallana, of whom sought his head for the killing of their father King Dhatusena. And more importantly, for usurping him as the rightful heir to the throne.

The site was also the setting for Duran Duran's 1982 video for 'Save a Prayer.' Just saying.

In the name of preserving one's sanity, when it comes to tourism it's generally always advised to avoid the weekends, that's virtually an international given. Unfortunately, I was here on a Saturday, and on my part it was just bad timing. And in any case, if not now, then never. And so thus, after paying a mandatory foreigner fee of $30 US, one gets to enjoy the delights of a monotonously slow, unpleasant and crowded single file trudge to the rocks summit; amongst a contingent of non-queue conforming Chinese tour groups, a barmy army of selfie sticks and innumerable quantities of fat crying children and fat crying adults alike. I too considered shedding a tear as the midday heat began to inject its might. However, somehow the King's big boobed concubine frescoes on one of the western wall faces for just about the briefest of moments diverted my abstract misery from the onslaught of over-tourism. For it wasn't long though before the full on assault continued, where I was to be sweated upon by strangers, harangued by a pugnacious wasp and informed by a spherical young American tourist in front of me that his butthole always chafed in such particularly compelling climes. This, like all over sold tourist attractions across the globe was all in order to get that pivotally important picture of other people taking pictures of other people trying to take a picture of somebody else taking a picture of somebody else taking a picture of somebody else trying to take a picture....of the back of somebody's head. Oh tourism, you sardonic bastard. Something told me that back in 1982, Simon Le Bon never had these kinds of problems (And I bet his butthole didn't chafe either!). Regardless, I found myself going through the motions, manhandling my way to the rocks summit before getting that compulsory tourist tick and then being back on my way; really none the wiser.

Nevertheless, the quiet country roads back to Dambulla somewhat remedied the day's indurate graft of tourism. Taking the edge away from a feeling that might even have possibly been deemed neighbourly to that of stress.

Back at the Welfare Centre, I stroked a tom cat and accidentally watched an Argentinian woman do yoga in a thong. All's well that ends well.

Dambulla - Polonnaruwa
53 miles

I awoke early to a melee of howling dogs coming from both inside and outside the welfare centre. Dogs I might add that had been so quiet and well behaved since my arrival, that it must've taken something rather remarkable to stir them up.

'*Sacré bleu*, dis is ridiculous, where is da manager?' Came the heavily accented voice of a largely disgruntled French woman. A smaller dog from somewhere yapped in reply to her demands. A door opened closeby to the debacle and the dogs instinctively settled down to the soothing voice of the welfare centres German manageress as she greeted the French guest and apologised for the raucous reception that she had received.

'Why is there dogs inside the 'otel?' The French aggressor demanded to know.

'Because this is my home and these are my pets...'

'You should not have pets in a 'otel.'

'I apologise but this is not a... hotel, it is a welfare centre.' One of the dogs let off a stray bark just to clarify the said point. I laid awake and stared at the ceiling for sometime as a war of words were exchanged between humans and canines alike. The fact this was all going on directly outside the door to my very room made my departure slightly awkward.

'But why do they bark at me? Is it because I am French?' And with that a vast and prolonged silence tore through the premises. Even the distant sound of traffic seemed to come to a screeching halt. It's quite possible that even Colombo some 99 miles away took a momentary pause to consider the questions gravity. For the atmosphere had suddenly become so tense that it could've been cut with a spork. I took this as my sign to leave. Gently opening the door to my room and with a series of slow and jaunty amoeboid like movements, edged myself around a clump of passing tumbleweed and discreetly slipped away to collect my bicycle. All as if nothing awkward had ever happened, nothing awkward at all.

The road conditions for the day: a hodgepodge of sublime beauty and raw brazen torment. For unwavering moments at a time I'd cruise with a remarkable air of dignity along an immaculately and freshly birthed road, before my easterly ambitions were to be subsequently ravaged by a series of potholed perversities. Still, for many a cyclist, to take the rough with the smooth is a necessity. And to complain, was forever futile.

Just north of the village of Bakamuna, along the winding Elahera Minneriya Yoda Ela canal, I met a couple of Dutch cyclists coming from the opposite direction. They'd thrown in the towel and had taken to walking their respective steeds along the rubble strewn track. Both of them were at least eight feet tall a piece, but probably more like 6 feet. Their flustered faces dappled with beads of sweat that beelined down their chubby cheeks like tears. We stopped to chat for the briefest of moments whereby they informed me to the miseries of the route that lay ahead of me. Whilst chin-wagging a truck shot past us at an alarming speed - caking us all in a foray of dust and pebbles. We all instinctively shook our fists angrily at the driver, of whom upon passing soon became nothing more than a gaseous puff of dirt and detritus. I was certain however that the driver was no doubt sat comfortably in his cab laughing his proverbial cock off.

I fought my way farther alongside the canal before a capricious change in road conditions intersected between Angammedilla and Wasgamuwa National Parks. Elephant fences aligned vast stretches of road as either side of me the rampant jungles reeled with life. In Sri Lanka, between the chaos of the roads that led to it's equally chaotic urban settlements, the chaos of the wilds are rarely but a stone's throw away.

I meandered along carefree and jovial, almost convincing myself that I was finally getting used to this sweating all over my handlebars lark. I wasn't, I was still technically dying; inside and out. But, if I could hoodwink myself with mind games enough to survive each day one at a time, then I would do just that.

As I drifted away from the jungle, the outline of a buzzard passed high above; it gracefully scythed through the thermals above a vast body of water - and one of the greatest achievements to emerge from the ancient city of Polonnaruwa.

14. Polonnaruwa
පොලොන්නරුව දිස්ත්‍රික්කය
பொலன்னறுவை மாவட்டம்

'Not one drop of water must flow into the ocean without serving the purposes of man.'
- King Parākramabāhu (1164 -1196 AD)

`Parakrama Samudraya, or the Sea of Parakrama: is a collection of five reservoirs inter-connected by a series of narrow canals that aid a catchment area of some 29 square miles. Its imperial architect and unifier of kingdoms, the 12th century ruler of the Kingdom of Polonnaruwa: King Parākramabāhu I. A king that took great pride in his land, of whom in his 33 year tenure at the top, was responsible for the construction and refurbishment of a multitude of canals, tanks and reservoirs across the country's dry zone. From building palaces, royal courts and Buddhist shrines, one of the last great kings of the island would carve an indelible mark on a nation for generations to come. And ultimately, became a hard act to follow. The Sea of Parakrama itself was his showpiece tank, capable of irrigating some 18,000 acres of rice paddies. It was during Parākramabāhu's reign, that the country was widely referred to as the "Granary of the Orient."

I edged along the sides of this vast watery expanse, as a delicate and consoling breeze flirted with my being. A huge water monitor lizard some 6 feet in length waddled casually across the road before me and slunk into the undergrowth. Away from the Sea of Parakrama, lay an ocean of lush paddy fields that nonchalantly swayed and rustled. The tumult of civilisation would soon be upon me as I closed in upon the central hub of this ancient city.

I found myself a sparkly new hotel of what must've consisted of some 50 plus rooms, yet seemingly only had the one guest: me. The hoteliers were merry enough to have me on board though, and helped me to unload my panniers from my bicycle and escort me to a cupboard under the stairs; that I would instinctively call 'my room.' I didn't linger long however, for I had some localised exploring to do. I returned to my wheels and went for a perusal.

As is the norm, there was a ramped up entrance fee for the foreign visitor: $25 US to free roam the sites. Then one is issued with a ticket that will be checked over scrupulously by a bunch of overzealous guards at certain checkpoints across the city; just to implicitly ensure that no one was getting completely and utterly mugged off. Now, as truly 'all templed out' as I felt after successive days of being drowned alive in a Golden Triangle of sweaty overcrowded sightseeing curiosity, I'm still at heart, a devout completionist - of whom still needed to tick that box. Just like I needed to cycle to every district in Sri Lanka - quite simply to prove something that means nothing. It was a bonafide necessity I guess, born of compulsion. Another self-righteous deed in an ever growing list that offered in return something along the lines of moral satisfaction, or was it actually the dream of everlasting escapism?

Yeah, whatever mate, shut up and just feed me some more of those sweet mindless factoids about the mighty 'Kingdom of Polonnaruwa' would ya? I sense you yearn, with an ebullient eagerness. Well, incidentally, I guess in part that's what I'm here for, so, one can indeed feed those sub conscious cravings...

After Anuradhapura, Polonnaruwa is the second most ancient city in Sri Lanka. In the 10th Century, the country then known as Thambapanni, was largely under control by the invading Cholas. After ransacking and more or less reducing Anuradhapura to ruin like a bunch of silly bollocks, the Cholas took it upon themselves to make nearby Polonnaruwa their home away from home. This sat uneasily with the islands principally Sinhalese populous. In fact, for the better part of a century they were downright pissed. Yet, come 1070 A.D, after a 17 year aggression, King Vijayabahu and his army quashed Chola rule across the country to re-establish power to the Sinhalese. And thus, the Kingdom of Polonnaruwa came to be. Over the course of the proceeding centuries the Kingdom saw varying monarchs come and go. It was King Parākramabāhu's reign however, that left an awe inspiring archaeological legacy for future civilisations to come. Even when the Kingdom eventually fell from grace in the 14th Century and the city was ultimately lost to the jungle, the bulk of his achievements as an industrious leader are plain to see some 9 centuries later. The glory days of the Kingdom of Polonnaruwa were now long gone, but what remains is a constant account of the past: from the royal palace to the council chambers, the towering Rankoth Vehara stupa, the 46 foot 4 inch long reclining Buddha of the Gal Vihara rock temple, the Vatadage: a circular relic house adorned with scripture, moonstones and guardstones that are said to have once housed the sacred tooth relic, the Shrine of Sixty Relics known as the Hatadage, and the royal bath, which once flowed with perfumed waters to appease the ancient monarchs. A pinpointed period in time that is still capable of inspiring future civilisations, allowing the imagination to conjure up majestic stories of the past. An open air museum that encapsulates to the best of its abilities the essence of what this great garden city once was; and a celebratory testament to the past at that.

Polonnaruwa - Batticaloa
61 miles

Come morning, and my bicycle lay in a calamitous heap - with a significant amount of scratches to the paintwork, a water bottle missing and ultimately and not least most insultingly, the entire bike was caked in cow shit. I scanned my surrounds. *What the actual fuck??* My mind instantly went to the idea of a thirsty and opportunistic water buffalo that whilst helping itself to the contents of my water bottle had decided to use my bicycle as a scratch post, and as a parting gift left some trademark sloppy buffalo defecation. And then suddenly, I was on my arse, seeing stars. My water bottle now by my side, which had just incidentally bounced off my skull like an intergalactic dildo of little to no remorse. I looked up, suddenly realising that the water buffalo hadn't been working alone in its act of blatant tomfoolery. For high up in the canopy of a palmyra, the endemic toque macaque, known locally as *rilawa* - was staring right back at me; *was that a sneer on its face?*

'You cheeky simian bastard!' I declared, pointing my finger at him with ruthless abandon. Well, I learned a lesson right there and then, as apparently, toque macaques don't take so kindly to white boys pointing the finger. For no sooner had I done so, did my newly founded simian arch nemesis bare his teeth and charge down the tree canopy directly at me. It was then, that instinct took me; I screamed wildly, and ran. Embarrassing myself in front of one of the hotel cleaners in the process. But I planned wholeheartedly on keeping my face attached to my skull, so to run seemed like the only realistic and viable option. The screaming part was merely a soundtrack to the occasion, and felt rightly justifiable under the circumstances. In hindsight, 'Save a Prayer' by Duran Duran might have been more fitting.

Once I'd ran out of breath, I turned to see the macaque skulking off back home up into the trees, again with my water bottle. 'Bah, keep it mate, keep it you thieving…-' the macaque swiftly looked back, and again directly into my eyes (not around them, in them!). I instinctively looked at the floor and apologised, realising immediately, my place in the primate hierarchy.

*

The eastbound road out of the city was hectic and dreadful. Clogged with hundreds of mining trucks filled with sand afresh from the banks of the Mahaweli - Sri Lanka's longest river at 335 km in length. This sand from the Mahaweli, meaning 'great sand' in Sinhala, and from the nearby settlement of Welikanda (mountain of sand) will be used in construction projects across the country, but largely in rapidly expanding Colombo. And, judging by the speeds incurred by that of the trucks that were edging past me, they were construction projects that needed constructing yesterday, and therefore not tomorrow.

I locked eyes with a central point upon the horizon, and focused, channeling out the melee of thrashing machinery. For to be caught under the wheels of one of these great hulks of lumbering metal, seemed all too easy.

The sky was to become overcast and capricious,

making the humidity all the more ridiculous than usual; giving way to the feeling of being suffocated by that of a dull and heavily soiled plastic bag. That big dull bag however couldn't hold out, and soon enough began to leak. Yet, after three weeks of uncontrollable and frenetic perspiration on my part, the fresh dousing was a welcome treat.

Alas, it was not all good fortune. For every little bit of content the road had to offer: sand, stone, grit, anonymous organic content and of course any available bovine poop becomes systematically attached to one's shins and bicycle components. The chain particularly susceptible as it made for a series of extremely clunky and uncomfortable gear shifts that every so often made me cringe with dread; like fingernails across a chalkboard.

I wondered if this was to be the start of the unpredictable North East monsoon season. It was hard to say, and I also wondered if Mother Nature even knew herself. Not that she'd answer to me, she never does.

15. Batticaloa
මඩකලපුව දිස්ත්‍රික්කය
மட்டக்களப்பு மாவட்டம்

"They used to say it looked like Eden."
- Father Dayalan Sanders

The lonely cry of a redshank rang out as the rain chimed sombre, delicate notes across the frame of my bicycle. Water dripped from my nose and traced the contour of my spine. There was something to do with the rain that made me think a little harder than usual. The rain, that for a while acted as a welcome relief, perhaps because like most days the sun wasn't cooking the limited contents of my brainpan like a hard boiled egg; and thus rendering me capable of actual thought. But rain being rain, is atmospheric in its very essence, and an ever ambivalent mood-setter. And it wasn't long before I came to question my being as a bog standard misery-clad simian, and more retrospectively my purpose up until this point - as a whole. The answers I found were generally a haphazard combination of vagueness, incredulity and denial. But thoughts and discussions that I felt were important to have with myself, because when you're on a long distance solo bicycle ride, thoughts for better or worse, are all part and parcel of the process. I figure that everyone, especially in regards to long-term travellers, they all have their respective reasons for biting off similar projects to that of my own. Whether that be reasons genuine, or reasons benign. There is not a one size fits all element to it. For some, perhaps it is to challenge ones attributes - their physicality, endurance, willpower or all round curiosity. They may be thrill-seekers looking for that next big fix, or dreamers in a land of possibilities. Retirees or recent divorcees finally looking to live their best life. Or then, theres's those lost souls, the socially displaced, the troubled minds; all looking for that great escape to aid the healing of wounds of an untold origin. We may come from similar pods, but we are certainly all very different peas. All however, are seeking substance to create meaning to their respective existence, that much is certain. But what happens when the quality of that substance begins to wane? What is it then that we become? There can often be an exceedingly sober undercurrent to the lifestyle of long-term travel; that not all those on short holidays, weekend breaks or day trips can associate with. I mean don't get me wrong, short-term travel or long-term travel, they are all still a gift to us, whereby we're lucky enough to be able to afford something so lavish in our lives. A self-reward for our daily toils. We are lucky fuckers in that respect. Truly. But, for those with almost chronic wanderlust, there is indeed a sacrifice to the cause, often inebriated by almost toxic levels of selfishness; especially in regards to solo travel. Careers can be sacrificed, relationships destroyed, children abandoned and the mind overwhelmed with thoughts and worry that may have never even existed before ones travelling partakings. I've seen on my travels firsthand the truly lost and it's not a pretty sight. The heart and soul of travel sliding to the wayside for any a long-term traveller is a danger. No matter how sane or on the ball we may regard ourselves, everyone of us is susceptible to the imbalances that can be associated with the road. And when/if the shit hits the fan, its pivotal to seek help, before eventualities turn pernicious, and therefore volatile.

As I peddled ever closer towards the coastal waters and lagoons of the Eastern Province, deep within the inner sanctum of my thoughts, I sincerely hoped that I had direction and therefore purpose, and that the equilibrium of my partaking was just - and I wasn't becoming lost within myself and edging ever closer to an unexpected mental episode. Maybe writing these words cements that to some degree, or maybe it doesn't. Maybe I'm just talking bollocks. But talking, that's a good thing. I know that much. Talking to ones self though? Well, that as ever, is very questionable.

Anyway, the show must go on.

Batticaloa, known by many as just 'Batti,' despite the damp, was a furor of drama and excitement. For Sri Lankan standards, a city of a modest size with a population of just over 92,000 citizens. The city's name stems from early Portuguese occupation, but its original Tamil derivation of "Matakkalappu," that despite sounding like an extravagant and new founded strain of STD, translates as 'Muddy Swamp.' Surrounded by Batticaloa Lagoon, the largest estuarine lagoon in the district, covering an area of some 162 square kilometres. It has been the lifeblood for many a generations of families in and around the city; from agriculture to aquaculture. An area of abundant coral reefs and mangrove forests that attracts vast riches of much valued biodiversity.

From Kallady Bridge, I cast an eye out across the lagoon. Amidst the drizzle, a fisherman in a small canoe hurled his net. Above him, a Brahminy Kite soared patiently in hope of a scavengers supper. In the waters below, folklore dictates that on a full moon between April and September, that the fish of the lagoon sing. Alas, it was currently a mid-afternoon at the back end of January and the aquatic orchestra was still seemingly on hiatus.

Just yonder, lay the small island of Puliyanthivu. An island that from satellite images resembles the shape of a turtle that is about to be dissected by an enormous landmass of claw. The island is somewhat of a central hub for the city with a thriving no thrills business district. To its north-east sits the smallest of the Portuguese/Dutch forts to have been built in Sri Lanka. Closeby, the colourful boulevard of the Mahatma Gandhi Park. Inside the park stands the Batticaloa Gate; a monument of stone arches where ships used to once make landfall from across the lagoon, and reportedly in

1814, the landing site of Reverend William Ault, the first Methodist missionary to Batticaloa. On a darker tone, at the centre of the island also sits the Zion Church, that just over a year from my visit became a site of one of the first terrorist attacks in the city since the civil war; and one of the six targeted locations to have been bombed across the island on that fateful day on Easter Sunday 2019. A needless killing of some 29 Church goers (mostly children) and the injuring of up to a hundred more. No stranger is the city to such violence, for when the LTTE occupied the city during the civil war for a bulk of the 1980's, it was commonly cited as being one of the most dangerous places in the country to have habituated. Again, hundreds upon thousands of innocent civilians lost their lives. And then, of course, came the tsunami.

I ventured on away from the hum and thrum towards Navalady; a remote and spindly finger of land that stabs out into the Indian Ocean. The tang of saltwater filled my nostrils as I cycled along parallel to the coast. The drollery of the hour saw to it that the ocean failed to sparkle. Its waters seemed agitated as it roiled and promoted a dreary haze of spray. The rapidly darkening horizon told me that the elements had grim intentions. My sojourn thankfully, was now within spitting distance.

On a small shred of land surrounded by a palmyra lined fence, there sat a wee place that went by the name of 'Soul Connection.' A rustic kind of place, crafted by charm and benevolence - with a steady reggae beat that drifted delicately across its foundations. I rested my bike up against a coconut tree. It looked dull and sandblasted under the grey skies and for the first time on this trip looked a little worse for wear. Come morning and I would have to give it a little TLC. But for the time being, I just couldn't be fucked. I felt worn and haggard; the wet having reached deep into my bones had inevitably sapped the energy out of me. Nearly as much as those sun-drenched days that were so often responsible for reducing me to an equal and mindless ruin (I said nearly).

Yet, if I could've been winding down anywhere on earth after a soggy day in the saddle, then I wouldn't have been able to find many a place more hospitable than Soul Connection. A gentle, dreadlocked man soon greeted me with a warm hand shake. His smile was both wide and infectious. This was Manoj, the laid-back and congenial proprietor of Soul Connection. He ran a strict 'Stress Free Zone' policy, as clearly marked by a signboard on the properties periphery. Manoj invited me over to a cafe-cum-lounge area. The walls were decorated with the vibrant artwork of passing strangers, each of their works leaving behind a trace of their respective auras. Positively charged auras that radiated and magnetised as an element of peaceful serenity encapsulated the surrounding confines. There was something here, something special.

As I sat, my soaked hair dripped water down onto

the bare sands beneath me. I clenched at it with my wet and shrivelled feet as the feeling of living in the now became suddenly so very concrete. I felt a wry smile counter my weary face. I was still completely bollocksed, but I was more than certainly at peace with it. Across the cafe from me sat a newly wed Alaskan couple, they both held knowingly warm smiles. They too must've felt it; for it flowed in abundance. It was invisible, yet somehow palpable. Manoj had orchestrated something special that could barely be described; but could definitely be felt. He also executed a mean curry and rice.

Batticaloa - Arugam Bay
72 miles

"The sea is coming!" Screamed Kohila Sanders, the wife of Pastor Dayalan Sanders. Roused from bed one early Sunday morning on 26th December 2004, the missionary had to act fast in accordance to save his wife, daughter, staff and the 28 orphans under his care at the Samaritan Children's Home. The orphanage sat between both Batticaloa Lagoon and the Indian Ocean; a precarious position as the ocean's blackened waters towered up into a 30-foot wall of devastation that surged forth menacingly. With no time to waste, the Pastor rallied everyone together at the jetty in order to ferry them all across the lagoon upon the outboard motor. And within sheer seconds of powering away from the orphanage, the quaint fishing village of Navalady was engulfed by the sea. For Pastor Sanders and those under his care that had already suffered so much, it was a lucky escape. For many however, their fate was sealed.

Some 15 years on and the tsunami still begat a sullen tone here. The orphanage now derelict, its whitewashed walls cracked and mildewed. Window panes shattered and rubble strewn. Where there was once life, there was now nothing. I walked into a buffer of pines that marched towards the coast. Not a creature stirred. A dark and eerie silence lurked forebodingly. Some 200 yards away and I could see the gentle lapping of water upon the deserted shore. I crept closer. And as I came to an opening onto the beach the silence broke to the mellow and rhythmic pull of the tide. There was a tranquil beauty to that moment, marred however by the memory of the 1,300 lives that were taken along this stretch of coast.

*

A briny drizzle descended on my journey south. The wet, consistent throughout the day, grew on me like moss. My thoughts again wandered. Bleak thoughts of what tragedies had befouled this beautiful island. The brutal hardships suffered at both the hands of man and nature. There are stories out there that are truly unfathomable and terrifying. Some of them disturbingly come with pictures or media footage that just can't be unseen. Sri Lanka's darkest of hours, I hoped, were at least now behind Her.

Alas, I was as irresolute as the weather and things had again turned mindfully deep. I started to hope that the azure coloured quilt of the sky and the searing heat would return to numb my roving mind. Stop thinking you horse's arse, just peddle!

16. Ampara
අම්පාර දිස්ත්‍රික්කය
அம்பாறை மாவட்டம்

'O Mankind! Behold, We have created you all out of male and female, and made you into nations ands tribes, so that you might come to know one another.' - Al Quran 49:13/14

And so, I took my own advice and shut the shop of my mind and I peddled forth; soaked and sodden. Through a series of wet and frantic settlements, that if it wasn't for the aid of Google Maps as a post-journey research tool, I would have most certainly forgotten their respective names: Periyaneelavanai, Sainthamaruthu, Addapalam, Addalaichchenai, Akkaraipatt, Sinnamuhattuvaram, Staines (Ok, I made that last one up).

In Kalmunai, the largest city in the Eastern Province, the lonesome wail of a muezzin filled the streets. A somewhat therapeutic calm wallowed amongst the damp. Displaced from Colombo in the 17th Century by the Portuguese, at least 8000 muslim refugees with permission of Rajasinghe II, the then King of Kandy, fled to the east - to settle in Kalmunai. Where today, muslims hold the largest demographic of any other town or city in Sri Lanka.

A desolate spit of land between sea and lagoon greets me at Thambattai. A vast expanse of seemingly infinite blue to either side. A soaked and scrawny looking white cow foraged amongst some vibrantly coloured sea facing tombs. I stopped to eat a couple of oranges that I'd purchased early that morning on the outskirts of Batticaloa. They tasted like xenomorph blood. And so I washed it down with some woodapple nectar, that in turn tasted like a sugary arm pit. I was all but certain that my guts were therefore entitled to a troubling night.

By late afternoon, I'd made it to Arugam Bay. Tourist season still at a low ebb saw many a hotels, guesthouses and restaurants on lockdown. In the rain, the town gave off a quasi-Cleethorpes vibe, albeit with palmyra in place of heroin. After some initial setbacks of being told that an empty guesthouse was either full or nobody spoke English, or nobody knew anything about anything, I'd eventually find a cozy enough ensuite cabana by the beach. Where, for the first time in my life I had a hot shower with a bicycle. My own bicycle of course, I'm not a complete slut. It took me almost an hour to scrub our respective fleshy and aluminium orifices clean. For the bugs and grime that my wheeled companion and I had accumulated upon our respective bodies were enough to warrant a new ecosystem.

It was dark by the time I'd finished and my stomach was screaming for food. Like seeking a place to lay my head, finding food was an equally challenging dilemma. If the shutters weren't down, then those establishments that I did find my way into seemed reluctant to fire up the stove. I eventually ended up in a Thai restaurant occupied by a couple of other foreign tourists with faces that each resembled that of an overly chewed Wham bar. Low season leftovers, if it doesn't kill you, it can all but make you stronger. So, I knew I was in for a treat. That was even before the charmless waiter tossed a menu at me and left me for dead for a good 40 minutes.

By the time he'd returned with a new haircut I placed my order.

'Green Curry please.'

'No sir,' the waiter waggled his head and also committed to something that was half-way between a wince and a sneer.

'No Green Curry?' Just to clarify.

'No sir,' just to re-clarify, with an ominous head waggle of re-clarification.

'Hmm...ok, well I'll just have to go for the red curry then I guess,' and that in theory should have solved that problem.

'No sir,' accompanied by a wince-sneer.

'Oh...just...no?'

'Yes sir.'

'And just to clarify, that was a 'yes' to the 'no,' correct?'

'No sir.'

'Perfect. Well, I guess it'll have to be the yellow curry then!' The worst of the Thai curries in my controversial mind, but still a treat all the same.

The waiter paused for a moment, before he offered

up a pristine of head waggle, wince-sneer combo to the tune of 'no sir.'

'Ah for fffu....nevermind. What currys do you have?'

'No curry sir,' confirmed and followed up with a well placed wince-sneer for good measure.

I felt a prickle of sweat attend to my brow, but felt that I was at least finally making progress with the curry situation. 'So, is there anything you can recommend to me from this menu?'

He looked about himself indecisively, I couldn't quite work out if he thought that maybe he was in some sort of dream and he'd just realised it, despite it however being a real world scenario, or, he'd just been nabbed off the streets an hour ago and hoist headfirst into the hospitality industry against his very will. He was certainly thinking on his feet, albeit quite slowly. He snatched the menu from my sweaty grasp. 'One moment sir.' He then disappeared for about 15 minutes. When he came back, he was freshly shaven. With notepad in hand he looked me squarely in the eye as if addressing me for the first time in his life and he said: 'Yes sir?' Followed by a what appeared to be a double wince-sneer.

Now I was officially miffed. What kind of madness was this? Maybe he'd hoped that the other foreigner had left and that in his strategic absence been replaced by another one that ideally didn't want to actually order anything because it may well entail a bit of an endeavour on the waiters behalf. Or was he just plain fucking with me? By this point I was so incredibly hungry that I could barely think. I turned and pointed at the other foreigners that had some how successfully managed to attain a meal and said: 'same, same,' which being in Sri Lanka didn't quite feel right, but allowing for the fact that I was in a Thai restaurant, I think it had some reasonable viability to it.

The waiter began to scribble something down. 'Meat sir?'

I took another look over my shoulder and saw the tourist couple still chewing away on what I could only imagine was the same bit of gristle they'd been chewing on for the past hour, and thus decided against it. 'Nah, just veg thanks.' He scribbled some more before walking away. 'Woh, hold up, a beer wouldn't go a miss.'

'No sir.'

'No beer?'

'Yes sir.' Wince-sneer.

'Yes, there's no beer?'

'No sir.'

I took another quick gander at the menu, I couldn't see any fluids. A fluidless Thai restaurant perhaps, the worlds first. I looked back at the waiter, 'water?' A note of desperation in my voice.

He waggled his head, gave a half-arsed wince-sneer and walked off.

I hoped for the best.

Fast forward 35 minutes and a slightly more jovial

and heavily moustached waiter appeared with a plate of fried rice and a bottle of water. 'Enjoy Sir.' Fried rice, a dish one can seldom fuck up and a cyclists staple that does exactly what it says on the proverbial tin. And it tasted every bit as glorious as my famished mind wanted it to taste. But then, I was desperate, such were the symptoms of my hunger, I'd have probably eaten a deep fried badgers ringpiece and declared it top draw.

Soon after polishing off my plate, the idea of a beer was something that I was finding hard to prise from my mind. To have that cool relief running down the strip and numbing my aches and mind collectively. Yes, booze would be my final challenge for the evening.

Farther down the street, I found an off license come bar. The local drunks were out en masse; amongst a dingy and dimly lit scene. An old flickering television amplified dissonantly in the corner of the room and offered a grainy glow to the surrounds. Some melodramatic Sri Lankan soap opera played out. Those that weren't passed out had their eyes fixated upon it. I made my way between the tables and towards the bar among a haze of cigarette smoke that choked the air with a dominant grip. The place yielded pissheads of the very highest calibre. One fellow had his face pressed tight to the table top, where he drooled like a newborn. Another laid back with his arms folded and his head sunk upon his chest; he snored in luxury. The bar itself swamped the bartender and made him look as if he were nothing more than just a floating moustache with a bit of cranium attached to it. I arched my neck over the bar slightly to confirm that he was more than just haunted facial hair. He was contentedly whole, and my mind was put to rest. His beady eyes that were set back deep inside of his head greeted me with a silently vehement gesture of 'Yeah, what?'

I peered at the fridge behind him. There was a choice of 8.8% Lion Strong, or 8.8% Lion Strong. 'Lion Strong please mate.' He pulled a bottle from the fridge and placed it in a plastic bag. I guessed I wouldn't be sticking around.

'600 rupees,' he demanded as he fingered his wooly moustache with pride. That was the best part of £3. I could get cheaper beer in Skegness. Clearly he was ripping me off. Yet, at that very moment I just wanted a beer with minimal fuss attached to it. And thus, I paid over the odds and was soon on my way, making sure to side step the newly introduced puddle of vomit by the exit.

Back outside and the cool night air washed over me. I cracked the bottle top off against a metal railing and took in an encouraging mouthful of beer. It was piss warm. I hated piss warm beer. I also remarked to myself that it tasted like gnats piss, the gnats piss I'd never actually tasted but always assumed that I knew what it would taste like if I ever did taste it (...if gnats actually pissed). I took a few more tender and disappointed sips on the walk back to my cabana, before reluctantly donating the remainder to an unsuspecting palmyra -

probably killing it in the process.

That night as the waves crashed along the shore and a cacophony of beach dogs hollered and brawled amongst themselves, I dreamt of an abundance of free-flowing ice cold beer that flooded my body without any iota of moral intention. Between then and eternity, there would be very few finer dreams.

Arugam Bay - Ella
86 miles

At dawn, in this surfers Mecca of point breaks and crashing waves, the sun glinted across the ocean like a molten sheet of lava. The skies were now clear, and whatever had unsettled the atmos over the past couple of days had come to pass.

I failed to find any cafes that were open for breakfast, but did make use of a convenience store in order to stock up on bananas and ginger nut biscuits; compulsory fuel for the road ahead. For today, I ventured back into the hill country, and fuel was more important now than ever.

The road out west to Monaragala, beyond a sea of rice, would see me traverse through lagoons where buffalo idly lazed, and to farther afield into ambient jungle, where hornbills screeched high above the canopy. I'd pass through Lahugala Kitulana National Park; at 1,500 hectares, one of Sri Lanka's smallest of national parks, yet home to a healthy population of at least 150 Elephants. Roadside signs warned me not to alight from my vehicle as a courteous passerby in a hatchback warned me of the dangers of elephants. 'Squishy, squashy,' he explained as he ground the palms of his hands together in a pulpifying motion.

'-Yep, thanks fella, I get it!'

I would see no elephants though, and was therefore grateful for the lack of all round squishy, squashy. Soon enough however, the road changed its geometry as a rugged and contentious wall of jungle scaled up into a dreary and fortified mist. And thus, I began my ascent, once again, back into Hill Country.

17. Monaragala
මොණරාගල දිස්ත්‍රික්කය
மொணராகலை மாவட்டம்

'Fujigraph' - (verb) to fudge around, waste time;
"Hey Anton, stop fujigraphing with that mikko bruh!"
                                                        - Sri Lankan English

By lunchtime, I'd made it to the town of Monaragala, a colourful little place dressed in billboards advertising all manner of mobile phone networks and real estate. Monaragala, the District, is the second largest district in Sri Lanka, and together with neighbouring Badulla they make up the province of Uva.

It was oppressively hot and I could barely count to four upon my arrival. And thus, found myself a little cafe amongst the shade to partake in the consumption of a soothingly ice cold ginger beer, a few samosas and equally, if not most importantly, to map out the route ahead.

Ella, at an altitude of 1,041 metres, meant that I still had a bit of drudgery to commit to; especially as I was currently only situated at a lowly 161 metres. The zigzagging of roads on the map were generally a cause for concern, for that meant a climb of serious proportions - and a bucket load of sweat.

I popped a samosa into my gob. Bliss.

Back on the road and my heart rate soon accelerated

tenfold as my quads powered on like resolute and fleshy pistons. The road twisted and turned as I rounded multiple switchbacks that were evidently designed by a mad colonialist on an acid trip. It was slow going and I rapped to pass the time. Why rapping? Well, I'm not exactly sure, as I wouldn't be seen dead rapping at sea level. But with the altitude, it felt somehow more assertive to do so; and in a way, more instinctual. Yet, what I rapped about I can't quite say, for it was also mid-afternoon, when I was at the height of my sunbaked delirium.

For a while at least as I continued on with my rapping ascent to Ella, the roads were pleasant and smooth. That was until I reached Passara - there they became painstakingly unreasonable and buggered beyond all rationale.

18. Badulla
බදුල්ල දිස්ත්‍රික්කය
பதுளை மாவட்டம்

'Perhaps there is not a scene in the world which combines sublimity and beauty in a more extraordinary degree than that which is presented at the pass of Ella.'
- Sir Emerson Tennent, 1859

I bobbed up and down the knackered inclined streets of Passara like a bucking bronco; amongst a deluge of fuming red government buses and a fit of rickshaws. People waved and shrieked at me and asked me where I was going.

'Ella,' I'd yell back at them. They would clap their hands and beam jubilantly upon my response.

For an entire moment it was a jovial slog, and I noted that I'd now hit the 1000 mile mark on my journey. This in itself endorsing a subliminal urge to high-five a passerby. The sun even fucked right off for a while as it became smothered by an ominous yet welcome grey cloud. The sight of a broken legged puppy though made me feel sad. And in this distraction, my front wheel fell haphazardly into a small crater in the road before sucker punching my saddle directly into the base of my bollocks. And just to truly offset the momentary grandiose mood, the sun burned through the cloud cover like fire burns through wool - just so that it might continue with its uniform task of sizzling me to a crispy husk. By days end, I would assuredly look like a giant, dirty Quaver.

Deep down however, I knew that everything was going to be just fine, as I still had a packet of emergency ginger nuts to rely upon.

Ella

South-westerly from Passara and the road thinned out to a narrow sleeve of busted rubble. The traffic had long since scarpered and the mountainside became my own personal struggle. It was a gruelling climb, and my legs felt like skin lined sacks of osmium as I scaled gradients that at times seemed to defy logic. My refusal to get off my bike and push as stubborn as ever. Yet, as I progressed higher up into cloud forest, the climate gradually became more bearable. The bird song that rallied out across the hills changed its tune, becoming more abstract; as a steady mist floated across the landscape and the air became thick with the scent of alpine.

At times I was blind to my surrounds, and then for the merest of seconds, Mother Nature allowed me a glimpse of her stunningly beautiful backyard; with her varying hues and mind-bending architecture. There were lush green hills that rolled boundlessly into the horizon and waterfalls that cascaded down into the unknown. Along with huge boulders that were spewed from the earth's core a millennia ago, where they sat entwined in thick trees roots that strangled them like face-huggers. Her inspiration was my fuel. I guessed it always would be. I rode on and on.

As I closed in upon Ella, it was early evening, and the sky was like a patchwork fusion of melted iris. An awkward descent led me down into the village, whereby my brakes screeched and moaned. The main drag through the settlement was heaving with life. Bar lounges, coffee houses and restaurants teemed with man-buns and short-shorts as a mixture of accents and languages from far-flung places blurted through the cool evening air.

I'd booked a hotel room in advance on this occasion. For the idea of cycling 80 miles into the mountains and then having to shop for a room at a reasonable rate was a deplorable one. The Nice Place Hotel was nestled on the outskirts of the village, down a long and winding dirt track; hidden well amongst a tea estate. It wasn't an easy find and I wondered for a while if the place even wanted to be found. Even the paunchy but admiral hotel manager seemed surprised to see me. More so when I declared that I had made a reservation. He waggled his head courteously, in it I detected tones of rigidness, delight and potentially a hint of fear. 'One moment sir,' he spoke softly, before rather abruptly barking something vulgar sounding down the corridor in the direction of an invisible force. There was a momentary pause, before a viperous response of a woman reciprocated with some words that sounded just as equally derogatory. The hotel manager or possibly assistant manager, judging by the way he was just spoken to, seemed embarrassed as he brushed a tuft of hair from out of his eyes. 'My wife,' he confirmed, 'sometimes not so nice lady.' I chuckled aloud. Had I just stepped directly into a Sri Lankan version of Fawlty Towers? He gathered a set of keys from under the desk whilst muttering some kind of Sinhalese unmentionable, before requesting that I follow him.

He led me to a large, airy room, equipped with a king sized bed and a balcony that overlooked an awe inspiring clump of Hill Country. My eyes widened. I'd only booked a $4 basic single and was expecting little more than a tussock of fabric in a cockroach infested cell block. I turned back to the hotel manager of whom no doubt noticed my enthusiasm for the view.

He smiled, 'upgrade sir.'

'Fine with me,' I declared.

'But tomorrow, you change, ok?'

I waggled my head at him just to make sure that we were both completely unclear about the situation.

He fought a smirk. 'You are very good Sri Lankan man,' he confirmed.

'Well, I do try.' I quipped. I did try though, I really did.

And on that note he bade me a goodnight and left me alone in my stately chambers.

I strolled over to the balcony. By now the light of day

was fast wasting away, and the rapidly cooling air demanded that I pull on my lightweight fleece. In the foothills, rickshaws whizzed about like fireflies as an ensemble of frogs began their evening recital.

My legs creaked as I took a seat. Had I overdone it today? Probably. Would I overdo it again? More than likely. Would I have it any other way? No. Just, no.

*

A I rolled out of bed my kneecap made an uncomfortable "pop." A pop that would become a keepsake, as it continues to give me issues to this very day. Clinical confirmation down the line insured that I'd definitely overdone it the previous day and more or less burned out the cartilage in my right knee.

Down on reception and Sri Lankan Basil Fawlty looked bedraggled; as if he hadn't slept a wink all night. I asked him if he wanted me to change room. Somewhat beleaguered he shouted something that sounded completely offensive down the hallway. And, after a deathly silence, a muffled female voice gave back some melodic, yet rancorously hellbent gyp that ended with the sound of a plate getting smashed and a picture of a gleeful elephant drinking a cup of tea falling off the wall from directly behind the manager. The manager didn't even turn to assess the situation with the elephant picture. It was clearly a bi-daily event that had become a standard.

'No sir, please stay,' he confirmed, much to my approval. 'Would you like breakfast?'

'Sure Basil, thanks.'

Over a breakfast of hoppers, a kind of pancake made from fermented rice flour and coconut milk accompanied by a mouth watering and if not slightly spicy coconut sambal, I watched from my balcony a hornbill butcher a jackfruit. It gorged manically as bits of fleshy fruit drooled from its heavyset and menacing looking bill. A bombardment of flies also pestered the exposed fruit and occasionally the hornbill lashed out at them in irritation.

Despite the contrasting views from my balcony, I grew restless, and the idea of me sitting on my arse all day grew wearisome. Therefore, I went for a walk.

Fast forward a couple of hours and against the screams of mercy from my clickety kneecaps I'd worked my way along an active railway line before finding a well trodden footpath that skirted far up into the hills. I'd pass through a combination of rice paddies, chili crops and tea plantations before finding myself at the summit of Ella Rock. The breeze upon this exposed section of hilltop chilled my sweat soaked body and made a shiver run down my spine. On a clear day, through a gap in the mountains known as 'Ella Gap,' it is said that you can see all the way to the southern coast of the country. The dramatic late morning cloud cover however challenged that supposition. But did in no way take away from the stunning viewscape that lay before me. The shadows cast by patches of cloud cover roamed guileless across the rugged hill country. And where the sunlight poured through the clouds it illuminated the land like a blanket of freshly cut emeralds.

Many a families, couples and friends that had trudged here, posed for pictures and celebrated with a victory picnic. A Dutch couple, Sasha and Thom, seeing that I was a bit of a loner, kindly offered to take a picture of me. Hesitant at first, I often dodged a camera about as often as I dodged a bar of soap. Yet Sasha noted that my mother would enjoy seeing a picture of me, even if I didn't. And she was right, on her mantelpiece in her living room, my mother still proudly displays the picture taken on that very day - haplessly making me cringe every time I chance a glance.

I descended back into town with Sasha and Thom, and we followed the railway line in the opposite direction towards Demodara. Here lay a manmade marvel to contest Mother Natures very own amply clad assets: The Nine Arch Bridge. A 91 metre long viaduct of nine arches that fills a void between the hills and connects the settlements of Demodara and Ella. When the colonial British first set out to build the bridge the Great War had started and thus resources, especially that of steel was reserved for the likes of ships, tanks, weapons, armour and ammunition. And so, local engineer P. K. Appuhami, set about completing the task using just locally sourced stone and cement. And to this day, since its completion in 1921, the bridge has stood the test of time with numerous trains passing along its tracks every single day.

Thom suggested we celebrate our walking exploits by going for a beer. Thom was clearly a man after my own heart. We headed back into the village and hit up one of the very many packed and trendy bars to accumulate the central strip. A bamboo clad affair with huge bean bags to sink into. We ordered three large Lion's and they were served up ice cold. My body ached every bit as it should have, but that beer, that sweet nectar of the Gods, it soon soothed those aches and pains immeasurably (Especially after five bottles). And thus we all chinwagged and exchanged fables from our respective lives until we were either bored of each other or just incredibly shit-faced, and then we parted ways - for an eternity.

It was nightfall as I stumbled carefree and numb through a forest in the dark back to Sri Lankan Fawlty Towers. There was a smell of smoke in the air that trailed from a distant bonfire as shadows whipped and stretched through the darkness in the lower reaches of the canopy. Farther up in the hills someplace, Buddhist monks chanted a mantra that merely added to how relaxedly rat-arsed I was. The reception was empty as I passed through on my way to my room. The picture of the cheery elephant drinking a cup of tea was hung up and back in its rightful place. I wondered if the owners of the hotel had now kissed and made up. I hoped that they had. Or perhaps, the manager was out on a remote hillside someplace hitting his rickshaw with a tree branch. It was hard to say.

Once back in my room, I crashed upon my bed and unfolded my map of Sri Lanka. I'd do well to plan the following days continued ascent into the mountains. Bleary eyed I tried to focus on a series of jaunty lines and unfathomable place names that didn't quite seem to want to stay still. I closed my eyes for an intentional moment.

Ella - Ohiya
24 miles

I awoke with a map that covered my face and a head only slightly more broken than it was some eight or so hours previously. But none of that shit really mattered as a decision had already been made for me - by myself no less. I was to stay as elevated as possible, and to ascend a further 800 metres up into the mountains towards Ohiya.

I told Sri Lankan Basil Fawlty my plans as I installed my panniers onto my bicycle in the lobby. He laughed heartily like I was some sort of ludicrous half-wit before shouting something unassailable down the hallway to his other half.

Pause.

Then laughter, slightly banshee-esque.

I too laughed along, pretending for no reason that I was in on the gag and wasn't just merely the brunt of it.

As I began to wheel my bike out of reception, Sri Lankan Basil Fawlty asked for a picture as he pulled out his phone.

'Sure,' I agreed and struck an uncomfortable pose next to my bike.

'No sir, me!' Said Sri Lankan Basil Fawlty, quite matter of factly; as if I should have known what he wanted. He opened up the flap to the reception counter and began to walk over towards my bike. Disappointingly, his stride was neutral and well paced. Nothing like the Ministry of Silly Walks-style goose step that I had half-imagined, or desired for that matter.

He briskly prised the handlebars away from my grip.

'Oh, a picture of you…..and my bike.' And then handed me his phone. He struck a pose. A much better one than I may have struck I might add; he was obviously a natural. I took a couple of snaps and gave him his phone back. He checked them over scrupulously.

'No sir, please take again.'

'Oh, no good?'

He smiled and waggled his head, that was definitely a *no*. He was very upfront and honest, I could've almost admired that about him if an 800 metre ascent wasn't awaiting me.

I'd spend the next 10 minutes trying to become National Geographic photographer of the year, until Mr Fawlty was content enough to allow me to leave.

The graft was soon upon me though and my

struggles prevalently real. As I ascended farther up a steep and winding road that appeared to serve the upper stratosphere. In the thin mountain air the filthy, jet black noxious fumes persistently chucked out by that of passing rickshaws lingered; making the air at times difficult to breathe. My right knee-cap also felt the burn as it gave off the impression that it needed to give birth to something quite unholy; if not sacrosanct.

Gradually, and little by little, the climes dropped. Even more noticeably so as I worked my way into a shady cluster of eucalyptus. And as the area became more remote and distant from the township of Ella, the tourist filled rickshaws petered away until a welcome silence clung to my surrounds.

I wrestled on with the ever narrowing, ever steepening mountain trail as my rapping became more fluid, more...intense. Occasionally a break in the tree cover offered glimpses of cascading evergreen forests and tea plantations that crept in and out of the swirling mists like the most beautiful of hauntings.

Amongst the forest a small train station emerged that signalled my arrival in Ohiya, and just further up from here one last climb to my pre-arranged homestay at the Green View Bungalow.

A chunky dog made sure that my hosts were fully aware of my arrival - barking excitedly as I rode along the properties jutted driveway. A couple with warm smiles greeted me by a cutesy bungalow perched not too far from a cliff edge. Across yonder, lay splendiferous views across the carpeted green sublimity of the Hill Country.

I dismounted from my bike and the overly friendly dog began to hump my leg. Presumably to congratulate me on my days feat.

'No, no, no, no….' the dogs owner came running over and chased off my newfound furry friend. 'So sorry-,' he proclaimed, '-he just very happy to see you. My wife and I also.' I looked around at the sex-starved canine, of whom was now trying to hump a roughly cut tree stump. *Not that happy,* I hoped. Yet the promise of a cup of tea and a plate of biscuits soon eased any such apprehensions.

The bungalows interior had recently seen a new lick of paint as the faded scent of fumes still vaguely lingered. Wooden shutters acted as windows and the tile floors shone proudly underfoot. In the living room a couple of children; a sister and a brother. They lay on their stomachs with crayons and drawings sprawled around them. On the arm of a chair a grumpy looking cat kept watch. At a large dining table sat a grey bearded man reading a book titled 'Birds of Sri Lanka.' The man introduced himself as Gheorghe, an ornithologist from Romania. Being a bit of a part-time birder myself I felt more than obliged to join him for a cuppa.

As we spoke of all things feathered and downy, an inexplicably divine scent of spice and herbs wafted over from the kitchen. Georghe's nostrils twitched and he began to stroke his wily beard with glee. 'The food here is quite magical,' he declared, with a puerile twinkle of excitement in his eyes. 'Tonight, you will not be going to bed hungry!' My stomach screamed as if to signal its inner most tenacious of desires. I then felt my left hand mischievously close in upon my chin, before giving my lacklustre beard an equally delicate stroke. This chin stroking malarkey was clearly contagious as I detected a wry smile creep forth upon my face.

And a feast it was too; potato curry with roasted okra and sautéed vegetables, with a dessert of *rulang aluwa*, a kind of mouth watering toffee of sorts. Even now, when I think of that mountain feast I still scratch my beard with a cordial sense of culinary completionism. It was a feast whereby you could almost taste the heart, soul and pride that went into it. From a lineage of perfected family dishes passed down from one generation to the next.

For on that night, I most certainly did not go to bed hungry. But on that night, in the darkness of the hill country, mystery lurked.

Ohiya - Nuwara Eliya
26 miles

The temperature at night dropped rapidly and I was glad to have been snuggled deep under a warm, thick duvet; hidden away from the cold, the leg-humper and any potential hill country tomfoolery - or witchcraft. For in the dead of night from somewhere deep within the forest, a drum beat arose; not altogether to dissimilar to those associated with the impending drumbeat of the invading army of orcs in the Mines of Moria from the Lord of the Rings. A mantra of chanting voices soon followed suit. There was undoubtedly an eeriness to it, yet somehow it was overwhelmed by the soothing ability of the very mantras simplistic nature. For all I knew I could have been lined up for a sacrifice. But it didn't matter, because the mantra was so calm and its drumbeat so suave that the need to escape was by all means inconsequential. I merely lost consciousness and allowed myself to drift along with the beat and into the cool night air.

Come breakfast, my hosts looked at me blankly when I enquired about the midnight mantras. My 'Wicker Man' reference only added toxicity to the confusion. None more so confused than my under the table leg-humping friend, of whom had taken it upon himself to resume business the moment I had sat down for breakfast.

Getting information in Sri Lanka was at times a rather nebulous affair, therefore I dropped the topic; saving face and all round embarrassment for all involved. Perhaps it was all just a dream, it had after all been a long and arduous day in the saddle.

There was just one other small item of note however, where was Gheorghe the Romanian twitcher? If his absence was for the Greater Good, I guess I'll never know. But when there was a breakfast of angel-dust sprinkled roti and spicy as sin sambal with sweet coconut sugar balls to go...who bloody cared?

My delightful hosts waved me off as leg-humper chased me up the driveway and several hundred metres along the road, before coming to an abrupt halt at the foot of an inhospitable and downright disgusting incline. He was a sensible leg-humper, I'd miss that filthy little bastard.

I took a deep breath, before piling straight into what felt like a sisyphean struggle of the most epic proportions. The dense canopy of the trees my only saving grace from the broad daylight that sought to penetrate with its ferocity. Needless to say, I rapped hard and I rapped fast.

I dripped sweat for fun,
My leg muscles throbbed,
My pants were knackered,
and my knee crunched like crackling!

I could almost feel the Gods laughing down upon me as I took a short break from a drossy rhyme to create something even more mildly ridiculous with my slightly aberrant state of mind...

Lord Buddha was taking some time out from sleeping on the job to have a peek at the unheavenly Kingdom of Earth on his Digibox. 'Hey Rama, check out this cycling bozo!' Shouts out Buddha as he flicks to recline mode on his La-Z-Boy and cracks open a can of non-alcoholic toddy; freshly brewed in the seventh layer of Nirvana.

Rama, King of Ayodhya, merges through a cloud of infinity, polishing his bow.

'Yes bro, this guy is freaking hilarious. Sita and I watched him yesterday get leg-humped by a mongrel.'

'This fool is good value for heavenly tax-payers money, that's for sure,' quirks Buddha.

'CAN I KILL HIM?' comes a cold and echoey voice from somewhere between above and not quite so slightly below.

'Oh, Brother Death,' sounds Buddha, slightly startled. 'I didn't see you there… lurking in the murkiness of yonder.'

A cold and sombre tone highlights the room as Rama suddenly regrets not wearing a t-shirt.

'WELL, CAN I?' Demands Death like an impatient brat.

'Erm..I...-' Buddha tries to tread carefully, '-one feels it is not quite appropriate at this time.'

'OH FOR GOD'S SAKE, YOU NEVER LET ME KILL ANYONE!' Said death sulkily.

'Oh do come along Brother Death,' interjects Rama. 'Buddha and I are having far too much fun watching this wallies show. It's like a B-Movie that's not meant to be funny but somehow is. You'll get your chance to end this simplistic mortal, just not today. '

Death tuts nonchalantly to himself. 'YOU REALLY MEAN THAT?'

'Of course, good things come to those that wait remember?'

'PINKY PROMISE?' A mischievously spindly and skeletal husk of a pinky appears before the Gods from out of thin air.

'Yeah, nice try Death, you cock!' Says Buddha sardonically.

'Well, it was worth a try,' quips Death.

'Oh look, he's made it to Horton Plains,' points out Rama.

'Oh my Buddha,' declares Buddha. 'Well, back to it I guess, later bro.' As he trades in his booze for a lotus flower to look more official and begins to float up, up, up and away to some place relentlessly dreamy and ethereal.

'Until next time my brother,' says Rama as he too fades away. The Gods hastiness to getaway from Death almost too obvious.

'OK, SEE YA LATER GUYS....GUYS?' And then Death was all alone. Just as he always had been. And, just as I normally was, just me and my imaginarium and an impassioned doggedness that saw me ascend forth through an ambient cluster of mountain chains highlighted by a well-rounded combination of great natural beauty, frenzied rapping and a collective of ludicrously non-biased, massively impartial God-fuelled scenarios that shall never come to be. Using this most unmethodical of formulae, undoubtedly saw me well on my way to the highest point I'd reach on my cycle tour of Sri Lanka. At 2,300 metres above sea level, my knees were reduced to ruin, but a signboard welcoming me to Horton Plains National Park saw a tinge of relief flood over me.

The park's original name Maha Eliya Thenna, meaning "Great Open Plain," was stripped by the colonial British in 1834 in favour of the then governor of Ceylon, Sir Robert Wilmot Horton. It would take over a century until 1969 for the 3,169 hectare site to be declared a Nature Reserve, and then, later in 1988, it was bumped up to the status of National Park. And, just over two decades on from there, in 2010, it became a UNESCO World Heritage Site.

From this tabletop plateau the headwaters of the rivers Mahaweli, Kelani and Walawe feed the lowlands of the country. A significant number of endemic species occupy the region, and up until the 1940's the area was home to a herd of elephants that lived at the highest altitude of any known elephant on earth. That was until the British did that thing that they so fondly used to commit to: murder.

The terrain levelled and expressed itself like a mountain top savannah, with spindly wet meadows, stagnant bogs, lazy brooks and lonesome moors. The redolent mountain air was frigid as a dense mist held camp on the periphery of a distant montane woodland. A non too plussed Sambar Deer grazed by the edge of the track, paying me little heed as I passed.

For a while, the dirt track meandered dutifully across the serene plateau without a soul in sight. A contrast stripped of its dignity some mile or so later as I rounded a stunted hillock to reveal an ocean of rickshaws and marching tourists. It appeared that the bulk of sightseers came from the north, in the direction of Nuwara Eliya. Thus meaning that my journey onwards from this point, was to become one mired by heavily trafficked and narrow roads.

I had however reached the beginnings of the World's End trail; a nearly 6 mile round walking route that would act as my overly active pit-stop before continuing my passage north. The track, through a swathe of cloud forest was well trodden as I passed a number of slow moving flip-flop trekkers before clashing head on with a Chinese tour group, of whom seemed absolutely committed to walking in the opposite direction to everyone else - all whilst listening to an awful racket via a cheap and cheerful ghetto blaster; presumptively to drown out the much sought after sounds of nature in one of its finest hours. A feat that having spent time trekking in China that will always mystify me.

Amongst the trees, Palm Squirrels manically skitted from tree to tree along delicate looking branches as a troop of Purple-Faced Langurs lazed around in the canopy; presumably avoiding the audible atrocities of Chinese pop music. At a break in the trees a rocky outcrop was exposed before a vast wall of whirling mist, that seemed to tussle and fold in upon itself in a state of atmospheric confusion. A small sign advertised 'Little World's End.' I walked to a stoney threshold and looked out into what appeared to be a gaseous, endless void. There, amongst a small gathering of tourists, I waited patiently. For none of us had come all this way for nothing. We'd all seen the pictures, now we wanted the reality of it all in its full and uncensored glory. Another Chinese tourist group soon appeared into the fold; cack music playing for all to hear. Several tourists in the crowd groaned. Everyone was soon however overwhelmed and any cultural differences put aside as the blanket of mist suddenly relinquished to reveal a cascade of green that slipped down some 270 metres into an expansively lush valley.

'Wooohh!' Expressed a chorus of international tourists; almost in unison, followed by a corresponding chuckle. I suddenly found myself stood next to a spine tingling sheer drop. Down below, amongst the myriad of green I could just about make out a series of Lego-like houses and farmsteads that dotted the range. A view that extended across both Uva and Sabaragamuwa Provinces. Alas, there was little time to get too familiar with such a spectacle before it was blotted out by the returning mists.

Farther along the trail lead to World's End itself. Again, with a little perseverance, the grand reveal is possible. But from here the 870 metre drop made for an evermore dramatic 'WOOOOHHH!!!'

It is a landscape undeniably spectacular, and far contrasting from the country's scorched salt-pans, its endless jungles of the Vanni or miles of palm clustered shores. Such was the beauty of this spectacularly diverse country with its seemingly effortless ability to charm.

I traversed farther along, amongst the company of giants: over my left shoulder Kirigalpotta (2395m), and to my right, Totapola (2357m); second and third highest mountains respectively in Sri Lanka. I'd also pass through Pattipola, which at an elevation of just over 1,897 metres, is the highest train station in the country. Thereafter, the endless verdancy of rolling hills became adorned with pastures of pristine industry standard ryegrass. Here, herds of Fresians and Ayrshire cattle grazed. I had now entered into the milky heart of Sri Lanka's dairy industry.

19. Nuwara Eliya
නුවරඑළිය දිස්ත්‍රික්කය
நுவரெலியா மாவட்டம்

*'Yes, that's it! Said the Hatter with a sigh,
it's always tea time.'*
— Lewis Carroll, Alice in Wonderland

At Ambewela, it felt like I'd taken the bizarrest of wrong turns and ended up in a distant, but not too unfamiliar land. For the area, with its immaculate green pastures, dotted with an array of patchwork bovines was nothing short of a blatant rip off of Hobbiton. Which in all fairness is rather unsurprising when locally it is often referred to as "Little New Zealand." The only thing the place was actually missing were Hobbits.

For many a years Sri Lanka has relied heavily on its milk powder imports; a traditionally more viable option in a country that hasn't had the infrastructure, stability or financial assets to support such a multimillion dollar industry. Yet, in recent times with a future seemingly less volatile, some of the biggest Western key players in the dairy industry from the U.S, Australia, New Zealand and Switzerland have all come to the table and invested heavily in Sri Lanka. A potentially controversial investment in an age where scientists are trying to convince the world to halve its dairy consumption to help offset the acceleration of climate change. But then who can really derail the wheels of mass-consumerism? It would take a a prolific stance in order to do so, and even then, money still trumps. And furthermore, milk is nice! Also, consider Sri Lanka's 483 million litre milk output for 2017; now naturally that sounds like a shit tonne of milk, but then compare that to the 91.3 billion litres that the U.S harvest annually and it becomes hard to reason why Sri Lanka shouldn't have a small slice of that curdy corporate cheesecake.

Away from the cows, the land turned more coarse, eventually giving way to the return of the plantations. Geographically, Nuwara Eliya has long been considered the capital of tea country; with its countless tea terraces that for the better part of 200 years have piled up high into the stratos; like a bushy game of Jenga. The estates are all very English sounding: Warwick, Norwood, Annfield, Somerset, Warleigh, Sinclair, Abbotsleigh - to name but a few. And, up on those distant slopes a vibrant array of multi-coloured dots represented the sarees of the plantations chiefly female workforce. There, for around $4 a day, these mothers, daughters and wives work their fingers to the bone. Many of them descendants of Indian Tamils that were brought over to the island from Tamil Nadu by the British; specifically to work on these plantations. For many, they would have lived a life consumed by a stateless existence. In fact, it wasn't until 2003, that a law was passed whereby any stateless persons of Indian origin that had lived in Sri Lanka since 1964 were allowed to claim Sri Lankan citizenship. Life had been hard for these Tamils of the Hill Country, and unequivocally it still was.

Nuwara Eliya, was settled back in 1846 by Londoner Samuel Baker - a known explorer (yay!), writer (yay!), naturalist (yay!), abolitionist (yay!) and big game hunter (Boo! - What a cunt!). For the British colonialists, the cool mountain air was of a majestic nature which endorsed memories of home. And, in a country with such savage climes it acted as a welcome retreat for many of the colonial bigwigs. The town, the highest in the country at 1,868 metres, still to this day has to it a quintessentially Anglophilian pulse. Something that it seems evidently keen on preserving. With its colonial buildings and country houses, a Tudor style red bricked post office with a red 'Made in Derby' post box. There are rose gardens and well kempt lawns, country parks, vegetable allotments, stables, a racecourse, cricket pitch, golf course and a clay pigeon range. Billboards around town even advertise property located in 'Little England.' And of course, the threat of rain is a near constant. Only hammering home its sheer Englishness.

There was still very much a Sri Lankan tone as the roads swelled with traffic that seemed to bleep and burp its way across town. Flags of the nation fluttered in the afternoon breeze atop colourful corrugated rooftops - held down by a combination of breeze blocks and knackered old car tyres. I passed bustling markets where the air was enriched with spices and the common profusion of exhaust fumes. A cow nonchalantly pressed through the bodies of people. Loud music blared out from somewhere, as a good-hearted argument ensued between a troupe of rickshaw drivers.

I threaded my way through some scruffy back streets and up a steep incline to find the Hi Lanka Hostel. A pack of feral dogs made sure everyone in the neighbourhood knew that I had arrived. Across an immaculate lawn where I could tell that its owner took great pride in, I parked my bicycle up next to a veranda. A few backpackers lounged around and eyed me with suspicion. I greeted them and they grumbled some sort of semblance for a cognitive response before returning back to the very international conversation of 'Game of Thrones.'

'Oh, but I suspect Theon Greyjoy's plonker was much less conventionally floppy in the books!'

As the afternoon progressed a series of black clouds loomed and it began to rain. There was no denying that as an Englishmen, there was a certain sense of home amongst the weathers inclemency. Therefore it felt only apt to put the kettle on and make myself a cuppa.

*

I sat on a bench. Not too dissimilar to Forest Gump. Except instead of a box of chocolates on my lap for my sweetheart, an assorted bag of extremely sweet cakes for my own personal lusting. I harvested them like a machine with very little remorse; a cake terminator you might say (but no-one ever would, why would they?).

The setting however was Victoria Park, a decadent

park of sorts, where Lords and Ladies would have once ponced gaily. Cleared and sown back in 1897 to commemorate Queen Victoria's Diamond Jubilee, the grounds today still gleamed brightly, all flowery and proud, and came as somewhat of a relaxant from the heaving streets of the town centre. And unquestionably, the best place in town to smash cake into ones face in public.

It would be fair to say, that I wasn't too far off from an all round park bench cakey climax when a man with a chagrined look about him approached my person. 'Do you know Queen Victoria?' He said.

I finished swallowing a filthy slice of perfection. 'Nah mate, a bit before my time.'

'She very fat no?' He was very direct.

'Allegedly, but I'd say she's shed a few pounds these days though'.

'No mister, she very fat, bye!'

'Oh, okay, bye then,' and with that the man walked away and out of my life to never be seen again. I have often been accused of being 'random' in my life, but that conversation was Top 10 material. I chuckled to myself a little before devouring a luscious chunk of sugary goodness. Divine. Quite simply, divine.

Nuwara Eliya - Nallathaniya
43 miles

The smooth and newly paved A7 westerly out of Nuwara Eliya was some of the best cycling that I would experience in Sri Lanka. Under a sky the colour of melted sapphires I'd pass through an endless cluster of tea plantations, amongst valleys dotted with waterfalls that spewed dramatically. For today, the fruits of my cycling ascent into the mountains were to be cashed in. I barely had to touch the pedals, being allowed to plummet almost effortlessly for some 20 odd miles or so; even reaching speeds close to my DWR (Doughty World Record) of 40 mph. It wasn't all glorious though, some of the switchbacks were spine tinglingly hair raising, and the big red devil government buses played their far from charming part to near excruciating perfection. When I wasn't getting stuck behind one of them and chugging on their fumes, I'd be breaking hard on a hairpin bend to allow them to pass me in order to avoid a head on from an oncoming bus in the opposite direction. Ordinarily, you'd assume the bus driver would only surely pass when it was safe to do so ...ordinarily. Even if the math(s) wasn't altogether too obvious, the equations of the roads here were different, and it paid heed to recognise and respect them.

Hatton, the largest town in the district was an unabashed riot of activity. And from what I could muster, its residents lived on a diet of carbon monoxide and scrap metal. Its geographical locale made it a gateway between Colombo and the Hill Country. Here I departed from the A7, that itself continued further west and down into the lowlands. The road that I now encountered was a contentious and buckled one, lined with all manner of nuts, bolts, oil, plastic, smashed fruit, anonymous scrap metal and 6 inch nails cast across the street that would threaten the very integrity of my Schwalbes. Yet, they remained stoic and reliable, and all so very efficiently German. I passed a smoking policeman stood next to a 'No Smoking' sign as a lorry flew past and buried us both in a miasma of exhaust fumes. I stopped momentarily to cough my guts up as an elderly lady approached me from out of the smog. She took a long hard look at my face before she held out her hand, 'money?'

I bobbled along through town as hastily as I could and away from the anarchy. Before long, I found myself ascending back up into the quiet of the hills. On the outskirts of Dickoya stood the empathic Warleigh Christ Church, that looked as if it had been plucked straight out of rural England. Perched on a hillside amongst a tea plantation, this aged and gloriously quaint stone church dates back to 1878; and still holds services every first and third Sunday of the month. Beyond, lay the scenically charming Castlereigh reservoir; where its still waters reflected the firmament above like a celestial illusion. And then, from there onwards I sensed that I was closing in on something special. It teased at first, like a mirage, before being shrouded in cloud cover. Something dark, something foreboding, yet all the same - something marred in a great and mystical beauty. On revelation, this caliginous figure loomed and entranced and seemingly drew me in - like one of its minions. Its outline dramatic, much like a giant bosom that fed the heavens, with an aura both grandiose and enviable. I cycled in silence; for to rap in its presence felt like a mockery. But there was no question now to what I was looking at: a pilgrimage.

Adam's Peak (Sri Pada)

*"If you have never climbed Sri Pada you're a fool;
if you've climbed it twice you're a bloody fool."*
— Unknown

I struggled to prize myself out of bed at 3 am, it always feels like such an ungodly hour to be committing to anything other than sleep or robbing a bank. Yet, through the gentile susurration of the water that flowed along my riverside accommodation, I swore that I could hear a drumbeat willing me to a attention. I was weary though of what lay before me. A thunderstorm had raged during the night. Lightning had outlined the shadows of a rugged and unforgiven landscape as a biblical deluge of rain fell. It was a surprise to me however as I exited my digs that the air was fresh and the ground beneath my feet firm and slush-free as I began my bleary eyed walk through the dimly lit streets of Nallathanniya. Muffled voices emerged from varying hotels and guesthouses; all jovial and eager.

For over a thousand years people have committed to this island's most famous of pilgrimages, to its vertiginous 2,243 metre summit. The mountain has many names and guises, all largely dependent upon each respective religions claims and interpretation of events. For the Buddhists it is the commonly known "Sri Pada," which means "Sacred Foot." This relates to a footprint on a boulder at the summit of the mountain, said to belong to none other than that of the Lord Buddha himself. "Adam's Peak," refers to the Muslim and often Christian belief that when Adam was cast from Eden for eating the forbidden fruit, he landed one foot first, again, on the mountains summit - where he remained one footed in an act of penance for a thousand years, and more than long enough to leave an impression. Similarly, "Sivanoli padam" - Foot of Shiva's Light - whereby the Hindu deity once trod leaving his/her mark. The shadiest backstory however has to go to the Portuguese Catholics, of whom stopped by in the 16th Century and claimed that the imprint quite clearly belonged to none other than that of Jesus's step brother, St. Thomas the Apostle; aka Doubting Thomas. Quite what such a doubter was getting up to ambling around in the highlands of Sri Lanka some 2000 years ago is anyones guess however.

Yet, regardless of beliefs and origins, there was no

getting around the fact that to reach the country's fifth highest peak, each and every pilgrim needed to commit themselves to a painstaking trudge of 5,500 steps. I felt personally, that after a month of solid cycling that I should've be fit enough for the task in hand. Alas, I still managed to sweat and slobber all over the mountainside like a sumo on a treadmill; as my right kneecap crunched away harmoniously to itself like a bag of broken digestive biscuits.

To start in the cooler morning climes though, was practically a no brainer. The path to the summit was well lit and dotted with a number of tea shops and snack kiosks. For myself, I'd come armed with an emergency can of tuna and a bottle of 7-Up. The ascent was a thrum of activity, where pilgrims both laughed and cried through the early morning slog. Groups sang amongst themselves and monks chanted mantras. My firm decision not to ascend-and-rap under the circumstances a difficult one, but no less an appropriate one. The young and elderly alike took intermittent breaks on the cold stone steps where passersby wished them good luck. All of them now knowing that the route that lay ahead was far from that of a painless struggle.

After a couple of hours, I'd filtered into a congested channel of pilgrims. A bell rang out from a temple to signify that another ascender had summited. I was glad to have made it. The summit was heavily populated as people vied for space upon a stack of concrete seating platforms, where they awaited for the sun to rise. First light though was still at least an hour away, and it didn't take long for the sweat on my body to chill. I threw on a jacket and ate my tuna. And then I, like many around me, shivered until the break of dawn.

I had just started to doze off or enter the early stages of hyperthermic shock when a raucous cacophony of awe startled me back to my senses. My eyes instinctively tuning into the other worldly apparition before me. To the east, a tear on the horizon that spilt a marvellous amber glow; like embers that burned through a painting of the night sky. A myriad of colours slowly crept across the canvas like an infection. The mountain audience stunned and close to near silence, apart from the occasional caterwaul of glee. It all seemed to unfold so quickly. And then, from over the crest of a mountainous ridge, the sun suddenly burst. A haze of distant peaks swiftly became apparent. As did mist covered cloud forest, distant stupas and a double rainbow to paralyze. A bird from somewhere braved a morning chorus. The cold that had crept through my bones just moments before had since left me, as the warm embrace of a new day went about its business. Another day had dawned, and it had done so in style. I wondered if there would ever be a greater sunrise in my life, or had that moment just peaked (no pun intended). But, if there was one thing that I certainly did know, it was all downhill from here.

20. Kegalle
කෑගල්ල දිස්ත්‍රික්කය
கேகாலை மாவட்டம்

'Oh-wo-ho, oh-wo-ho' - Glenn Frey

Nallathanniya - Ratnapura
77 miles

From Adam's Peak, one could have descended directly down its western slopes and trudged a 13 mile swathe of gruff jungle, through the Peak Wilderness Sanctuary and onto the town of Ratnapura - ultimately where I planned to end my day. It was an alluring and tempting feat, yet not a particularly viable one with a pushbike as a companion. And so by road, I would have to settle for a 77 mile detour around the mountains; that defended my entry to Ratnapura like a heavily vegetated battlement.

The roads were twisted and crumpled, and made for slow progress. My slaving aided by the imposing western slopes that lay before me - a beauty undeniable, yet a beauty unforgiving. In time the cool mountain air gradually ebbed as the prickly jungle heat bullied and intensified. In my head a song began to torment me: 'The Heat is On,' by Glenn Frey. Nevertheless, despite the vomit-inducing climes seemingly afresh from the Devil's bagpipes, I was statistically in the wettest region of the country. Kegalle district has long been prone to a near annual fatal series of devastating floods and landslides. Such is the capriciousness of the country's climatic diversity, the region bares the brunt of both of the country's monsoon seasons; as well as an inter-monsoon period. The south westerly from May until September, more often than not being the most catastrophic. The southwestern fringe of the mountains alone receives on average an annual rainfall of some 4,000mm of the wet stuff.

On this hot and dry February day, the Kelani River still roared mightily on my approach. A river famous for its white water rafting and the filming location for the 1957 classic, 'The Bridge on the River Kwai.' And as I Entered the town of Kitulgala, its streets were filled with signboards that all seemed to tout the best white water rafting experience in town. Tourists strutted about in wet-suits armed with oars and looks of trepidation written upon their faces; as the eddying waters of the Kelani beckoned.

At a pitstop on the side of the road, I drank some mango juice and what I suspected on appearance alone to be that of a massive samosa. Well, I dropped my suspected massive samosa into the dirt like a thoroughbred tosser, whereby it was swiftly polished off a by a street dog with multiple limps. On passing, an elderly lady with an umbrella, cackled and offered me a toothless grin. I smiled and reciprocated in kind by offering her a glimpse of my equally lacklustre British teeth. By all accounts, she was horrified.

The A7 was not to be trifled with, as it roared just as vociferously as the Kelani that ran alongside it. I shared it with a procession of gear grinding diesel guzzlers stacked precariously with epic hauls of timber. Concentration was pivotal, to lose it was to lose a limb, or worse. And in such climes, this level of intense focus soon depleted ones very will and integrity. Glenn Frey was by no means helping the situation; his volume seemed to increase in my head to coincide with the surrounding dissonance. In fact, it seemed only appropriate at such a point to sing aloud. And thus, I did just that. This small bout of oozing delirium somewhat eased the desire for me to toss my Ridgeback into the river and catch a bus back to Colombo.

It was only on escape from the A7's feisty torment that I found sanctuary, and that Glenn Frey had agreed to shut his fucking mouth (albeit temporarily). The roads quietened as I weaved my way along some intrinsic sections of backcountry; where the pace of life suddenly slowed. People snoozed in hammocks on their porches, or crouched in small groups by the side of the road where they smoked and shot the breeze with their neighbours. This was all much more to my liking. An agreeably humblesome side of Sri Lanka that certainly eased ones mind away from the grim ordeal of the A7.

Alas, just as I was getting used to this laidback amble, I came to an inglorious intersection of sorts, whereby a lorry the size of Ashby-de-la-Zouch rumbled passed and kicked up a torrent of dust that almost saw me tumbling into a ditch.

'Tell me can you feel it, tell me can you feel it, tell me can you feel it!'

I'd reached the A4, and on cue Glenn was back on lead vocals absolutely bossing it - like a boss. But I had at least made it to Ratnapura. That was something.

21. Ratnapura
රත්නපුර දිස්ත්‍රික්කය
இரத்தினபுரம் மாவட்டம

"We should not play like Austrailia or India or England - we should play like Sri Lanka."
- Mahela Jayawardene

After the indecorous spoils of both the A4 and the A7, with its panoply of thrashing metal and enough noxious output to choke a Russian Dwarf Hamster to death within nanoseconds, I was treated to a thunderstorm. It was dusk as I rallied into the peripheral cusp of the township of Ratnapura. Skewed shadows began to form around the towering palmyra as I cycled along an old narrow railway line that had been paved over and aptly named the 'Old Railway Road.' It was here that the sky truly tore open and that the heavens poured gratuitously. A cool comfort reinvigorated my tired body. A petrichor of freshly damp earth contended with an aromatic array of spices that exploded from out of the suburbs. As the low-light of evening transcended, television screens glowed among the dim, and cicadas from the surrounding bush sung to the rhythm of the falling rain. My senses gradually worked their way back to me and I was finally free from the shackles of monotonous 80's trash-pop (Sorry Glenn!).

Ratnapura is the capital city of Sabaragamuwa

Province. A congested town of haggling gemologists with dreamy jewell-eyed gazes all trying to broker that sweet deal of a lifetime. Ratnapura, meaning 'City of Gems,' is famed for its gem mines poised along the murky banks of the Kalu Ganga and its surrounding valleys. And so, it seemed only apt that the guesthouse that I sought was appropriately named the Sapphire Holiday Resort. As was so often the case with my evenings in Sri Lanka, I found myself plying a dirt track road in order to find my digs. As a rule, the cheapest and the most cheerful are often those that are tucked away and out of sight. And, just as the surrounding jungle began to grow darker and a knot of unwavering dread began to edge its way further through my loins, a floodlight suddenly lit me up; exposing me like a popped pustule. Through the blinding light a sign for the Sapphire Holiday Resort caught my attention. The hosts of the guesthouse soon rushed out to greet me warmly; as one might do an old friend. I would be their only guest for the night, in a guesthouse that possessed a unique jungle fusion decor. Crafted of vine and wattle, and various other natural materials sourced from the surrounding area. It was a warm and homely place, the food impeccable and the beer served ice cold - not always an easy find.

That evening, I sunk into the mattress of my rooms four poster bed and channel surfed through roughly 88 channels of cricket-porn. A procedure that enticed me to fall deep into dream.

Sinharaja Forest Reserve

My compulsory guide walked the mulchy path ahead, amongst a white noise of pure jungle euphoria. Great Vines hung down from aged trees and stroked our shoulders delicately upon passing. Some of these aged giants climbed upwards of 40 metres into the canopy, where they stood tall with a sort of urbane, if not woody pride at supporting the surrounding ecosystem.

The Sinharaja Forest Reserve is Sri Lanka's first natural site to make it onto the UNESCO World Heritage list. A dense montane rainforest that spans for some 18,900 acres. Bordered by three rivers, it ranges in altitude from 300m to 1,170m. A temple of life, from the Badger Mongoose, to the Ashy-headed Babbler, the forest consists of over 154 bird species, 139 endemic plants and over 50% of the country's endemic reptiles, mammals and butterflies.

For the occasion, my guide made me feel slightly overdressed in his light blue buttoned shirt, rolled up black jeans and a pair of flip-flops. In comparison, I wore khaki cargo bottoms, a long sleeved shirt, a wide brimmed sun hat and a pair of hiking boots. I was clearly representing the poor man's Indiana Jones demographic. My guide strode almost perversely through streams, across slippery lichen covered rocks and amongst tangled undergrowth; giving very few jots about the dangers that be, i.e: snakes, spiders, scorpions, leeches, thorns, air-barnacles, slips, falls and undoubtedly some Stephen Speilberg-esque booby traps. Despite his comfort in his attire though, I did rest assured that if we did somehow set off a trap and a giant boulder should tear after us down a ravine, then theoretically I felt that I stood a slightly better chance of escape whilst wearing my boots as opposed to flip-flops - just saying!

My guide would turn from time to time to point out certain key features in both English and Sinhala: tree, bird, flower, water, floor, Russian. He was a smiley chap with very limited English. But then I did pay bottom dollar for the experience. I never did learn his name, for when I introduced myself as Daniel his only response was 'yes.' He did relay to me in a charades like fashion however that he had three children and that they were all three years old and he lived in a small village just outside the Forest, where he had lived all his life for three years, with his wife of whom was also three years old. I presumed and hoped however that that last and marginally sinister fact was merely a breakdown in communication. I sincerely hoped so anyway. But for all intents and purposes I shall now call the guide 'Three.'

It was hard not to be mesmerised when one is so deep in the bowels of such a vivacious and biodiverse world An expansive biome, where flora competed for light and rare species skulked, fluttered, grew and murdered one another 24/7. It was a wet and wild place, not too dissimilar to a lost weekend in Croydon. As Three and I arched under a fallen tree and up a steep slope, I found myself tuning into the forests throng of ambient individuals. A mantra of leaking gas performed by legions of cicadas, the drumming of a woodpecker, the distant whoop of a purple-faced langur, the shriek of 'danger!' from Three. The guide held out his hand haltingly for me to cease my dreamy waltz. I froze like a Covent Garden life statue (a shitty one that sweated copiously). He pointed into a lime coloured section of scrub, where there was a neon like lump of vine with a bulbous tip draped around it. It took an ashamedly long time for me to work out what it was I was meant to have been looking at. That was until the flutey objects bulbous tip stuck its orange tongue out at me. 'Holy crap, a snake!' I jumped back, clearly alarmed as Three began to point and laugh at my dumbstruck face before he feigned abstract fear. He was mocking me. 'I...I wasn't scared, just...pleasantly surprised.' Clearly trying my very worst to defend my honour.

In Tamil, the snake is known as *pachai paambu*, otherwise known as the green vine snake, a common sight across many a forest habitat throughout South and South-East Asia. A diurnal species that lurks amongst the vines picking off various frogs and lizards. And although considered venomous, is of no particular threat to man. Regardless, I edged around its territory respectfully as not to tempt any unnecessary fate.

As the day grew on, the surrounds became increasingly moist and patches of upland forest began to haze over in a clingy mist. Leeches soon became a problem, and we'd often have to stop to remove them. The most common place part of my body to find them was on my feet, where they would somersault up from the ground litter and thread their way silently into the confines of my boots - before noshing off my flesh. I felt it fair to note that they were true forestry scumbags of the highest order. Yet, they were merely doing their thing, and to some extent, I felt that they were nowhere near as villainous as the lowly mosquito; Mother Nature's most vilest of acts.

'Fuck my face off, it's a scorpion!' Some hours later and Three had managed to do it again.

'Your face, very scared sir.'

'Oh, fluent in English piss-taking now are we?' Three simpered slightly as he put his lighter away. He'd just gotten me to stick a twig into a hollow in the ground, where something inside tugged on it at the other end.

'Look closer,' hinted Three, and as I pushed my face ridiculously close to the entrance of the hollow, Three lit his lighter to illuminate what lay within. Well, it was black and shiny, with pincers that could've snap a man's finger clean off. It was clearly a scorpion, that had a cold and solid clasp upon the other end of my twig, to which I instantaneously dropped at my end. I backed off instinctively in a state of alarm - all much to the joy of Three. The guy certainly knew how to get his kicks, I'll give him that. And for these aspiring cheap thrills, Three had certainly created bang for his buck. With his antics however, I'm almost certain that he'll probably get someone killed one day. In fact, he'll definitely get someone killed.

Ratnapura - Deniyaya
61 miles

It was dark in the jungle, and somewhere out there the crack of gunfire rallied. I was moving fast. Really fucking fast. Too fast. Vines pulling at my limbs and spider-webs like barbed wire tearing at my face. I find an opening that leads me to a saltpan wilderness. In a haze of heat ripples, an umbral figure walks slowly at a distance. *Romford*? I feel something rubbing against my leg. I look down at a nuzzling leopard. Its eyes are bright and wild, its paws the size of my head. I feel dumbstruck, like a rabbit in the headlights as it opens its great and powerful jaws to roar. It is then that I wake in a pool of sweat; wondering just what exactly the ingredients were that the chef had used in that so-called 'jungle curry,' that I'd devoured that very evening. But soon came to the conclusion, that it was probably for the best that I never know.

At the soft light of dawn, I crept away from Ratnapura with a vague notion of a plan. These notions that so often felt like they should've had harsher consequences. A brief glance at some squiggles on a map of a distant land and I was on my way with a kind of lacklustre ease that I'm almost certain would have any a loved ones concerned. The fact is, that when you commit to a venture such as this partaking, after a while, ones decisions largely become instinctively whimsical, as if ingrained by the trials of the road. It had become a job, whereby I didn't always have to think so much. This I felt was genius on my part, for thinking can so often become a downright burdensome peeve.

To the south of Ratnapura, lay the Sabaragamuwa Mountains and the wilds of Sinharaja; a natural divide between myself and the town of Deniyaya. The road that trailed away from town once clustered and anarchic, seemed to narrow by the minute, before it converged into nothing more than a scraggy and tasseled path. The mountains that rose before me skirted the eastern fringes of the rainforests of Sinharaja. I sweated and cursed my way along a stiff ascent of ten individually numbered and gruelling bends; locally called '*Wangu*'. The roadsides were however well shaded, under a canopy of pines that shielded me from the blinding ferocity of the sun. The road traffic was all but obsolete. Here, I could smell the freshness of the mountain air and not choke upon malodorous toxic fumes. I could hear the birds chatter amongst themselves in the undergrowth. Exotic flowers bloomed in yellows, violets and blues. As wild grasses grew rampant around huge monolithic rocks that littered the landscape. For a while it was an embellishment of true wilderness. That was, until it wasn't. It seemed to travel across the mountainside like a dreadfully lonesome wail. Amplified and terrifying. To begin with I was worried that someone out there somewhere was in great pain. Until I realised that the catastrophic whimperings were accompanied by a underlying beat. I'd soon close in upon a small farmhouse. Its doors and wooden slats for windows were shut tight through shame, but its very foundations shook under a heavily sinister bass beat, accompanied by vocals both heinous and somewhat possessed. This was jungle karaoke, the worst kind of karaoke known to mankind. I wondered how long the perpetrator of such an atrocity had been working on that ballad and how many lifetimes he would need to perfect upon it. Not that he would've heard me, but I bade him good luck on passing anyway. He'd certainly need it.

Farther along at a switchback, a couple of young men were sat together under a jackfruit tree; possibly one of the worst and most fateful places to hang out. If coconuts maim and kill an alleged 150 people every year, then I'm almost certain that the Jackfruit that grows to an average size of an enormous 16 kilograms, statistically shouldn't trail too far behind the murderous deeds of the coconut. As I approached, I noticed one of the young men was passed out cold with his head rested upon his friends shoulder. The one that seemed visibly alive, greeted me as I stopped to ask if his friend was alright. The young man giggled, his eyes bloodshot and wily.

'Too much smoke,' he answered.

'Ah right,' I replied, with not too much else to add.

'You want?' The young man smirked as he held out one of the fattest blunts I had ever seen in my life. I glanced at his comatose friend, a bit of spittle ran the flank of his smooth brown cheek. He was fucked up and probably would be for the next 9 years.

'Nah mate, better not. I'm driving,' as I motioned the peddling of my bike.

'Ok brother, no problem,' as he took a big hit of his doobie, and lay his head back against the tree and slunk down it like fleshy slime. I did fancy getting fucked up, but under a jackfruit tree in butt-fuck nowhere, half way up a mountain didn't quite seem appropriate. I cycled on.

Another delicate gloam was soon to breach, marking another full days graft in the saddle. I'd found my way down a bumpy road from the mountains, that felt more like a staircase, and into the inner workings of Deniyaya. There, a bakery-cum-hostel would act as my lodgings for the night.

22. Matara*
මාතර දිස්ත්‍රික්කය
மாத்தறை மாவட்டம்

Q: What animals are best at cricket?
A: Bats

Deniyaya - Tangalle
44 miles

It was a smooth descent south, along the A17 away from Deniyaya. The coast beckoned. As did a pissup. Yet I would soon be forced to work for my vice as I strayed easterly, along a hill congested series of B-roads. On occasion, the route became too steep to cycle, and I was left with little choice but to get off and push my load. The heat hammered me as I left a flash flood of sweat in my wake. I was spurred on by the village locals with cheers of support as I passed through the bucolic and respective settlements of Pasgoda, Mawarala, Mulatiyana and Deiyandara. This encouragement of strangers forever in my heart.

A cluster of trees filled with what must've been thousands of giant fruit bats halted my progress. They flapped and stretched their delicate and waxy looking wings as they bickered amongst themselves:

Bat 1: It's fucking hot!
Bat 2: It's always fucking hot!
Dave the Bat: I need a shit!
Bat 1 and 2: Oh, for fucks sake Dave, not again!

The inland air remained unreasonably static as I wiped reservoirs of perspiration from my equally unreasonable face. Yet, I remained defiant, for the reward in my mind had an almost undemolishble prowess. I could almost feel that sea breeze on my skin and taste the ice cold lager as it poured down my gullet. I just had to keep pedaling. It was as simple as that. In fact, as far as my life was concerned, I doubted that it would ever get much simpler.

23. Hambantota
හම්බන්තොට දිස්ත්‍රික්කය
அம்பாந்தோட்டை மாவட்டம்

'Like cutting off fence posts and throwing them into the river.' - Sinhalese idiom

Tangalle

As I sat on the beach with my second ice cold beer of the afternoon, all of the days sweaty proclivities suddenly felt appropriate. It felt good to be back by the coast. It always felt like there was a certain sense of achievement to be had at having a tipple after a bout of hard toil. My surroundings also committed to nothing more than milking the situation. Under a gently swaying canopy of palms I sat shaded. The sea, mere metres away, bounded along the shoreline with a delicate intimacy. Its waters mirrored the deep blue sky above as the sand upon the beach lay pristine and smooth; as if untrodden for a millennia. It was the finest of emolument. I drank until the mosquitoes confronted me. And thereafter, I drank some more.

*

I awoke with the lacklustre idea of doing exactly absolutely nothing. Something that I would largely stay faithful to. Not that Hambantota wasn't without its options; if a failed stab at commercialism was your thing. As the country's civil war drew to a close in 2009, the then 6th president and local lad Mahinda Rajapaksa, became hellbent on spunking billions of dollars in high interest Chinese loans (US$8 billion by all accounts!) in an attempt to make his home district a commercial hub of success. This ranged from a series of ventures that included an international seaport, cricket stadium, golf course, convention centre, botanical gardens and a string of sparkly new highways to tie them all together. But most famously of all, came 2013's international airport in Mattala - some 11 miles north of district capital Hambantota. An airport that before it even got the nod, had attracted widespread condemnation from conservationists, by virtue that it would destroy some 2,000 acres of jungle habitat; whereby amongst a myriad of wildlife, some upwards of 200 elephants would be displaced. That, and the fact that the airport was to be situated in a huge migratory bird flyzone surrounded by a number of vitally important wetland sites. Aviation experts also seriously advised against its construction - where they warned of malicious crosswinds that could potentially hamper landings and takeoffs of aircraft, and therefore present a higher risk of death to all those on board flights both in and out of the proposed airport. Well, 'bollocks to all that guff,' declared Mahinda, in no uncertain terms. He wanted a second international airport in the middle of the jungle, named after none other than himself. And that was just what he got. The venture would cost in the region of US$209 million, of which US$190 million was loaned directly from the Chinese government. And guess what? That's right, nobody came. The airport would soon go on to be dubbed "The World's Emptiest International Airport." At the time of writing, at the back end of 2019, there were no direct international flights and the couple of direct 30 minute flights to either Colombo or Kandy would set you back somewhere in the region of £400 - flights so ridiculously overpriced that it was almost a certainty that aircraft stay grounded. It did however keep the army busy, as in 2016 over 300 soldiers were employed to scare off the animals that had crept out of the surrounding jungles and encroached upon the airport terminal. The freeways that led to the terminal were now used by sunbathing dogs and local farmers to dry peppers. It had also become more lucrative to rent out the pigeon infested hangers to rice farmers as a dry storage space. And so, for an airport that boasted the ability to process some 100 million passengers every year, its waiting rooms were destined to sit eternally empty, its check-in desks to welcome no one, its well polished floors to slowly fade and its runway, parking lots and drop-off areas to be frequented by prowling peacocks. It seemed like only a matter of time before the jungle would reclaim its rightful territory. I for one sincerely hoped so anyway.

The problem is, in a district of just 596,617, whereby

96% of its inhabitants are classed as rural residents that made a living from fishing, salt production, rice farming and varying other agricultural ventures, all these brand spanking new acquisitions scarcely made sense. Especially when the only achievements to be garnered were all but negative; i.e a mothballed airport, empty golf courses, a seaport that the country could ill afford (that had since been leased out to the Chinese - all no doubt part of the masterplan), a cricket-less and crumbling cricket stadium now used solely for the occasional wedding reception, and a convention centre that quite frankly nobody gave a toss about. An interesting if not calamitous series of business ventures to say the least. But did I feel the necessity to visit these proverbial white elephants as a tourist? Fuck no, a 60 mile round trip just didn't seem warranted. Especially when I'd found a place where the beer served was so invitingly cold. I'd be spending another day at the beach, getting shit-faced.

22. Matara**
මාතර දිස්ත්‍රික්කය
மாத்தறை மாவட்டம்

'Mad? I am mad of course if to shape one's own life, to live it and love it is madness.' - Maurice Talvande, Count de Mauny Talvande (self-proclaimed)

Tangalle - Polhena
28 miles

By mid morning I'd reached Dondra Head, the southernmost point of Sri Lanka. I was now some 271 miles in the opposite direction from Point Pedro; the country's northernmost point. There was once a time when Dondra was the country's capital, where to its bustling port, it attracted seafarers from the farthest regions of Asia - to trade at the town's famed emporium. A town that also went by the name of Devi Nuwara, "City of the Gods." A place that saw pilgrims flock from far and wide to worship the Hindu deity Upulvan, the guardian of Sri Lanka. At the Tenavaram Kovil, some 500 women known as *devadasi,* served and dedicated the entirety of their lives to the worship and services of the enshrined deities. That was until 1588, when the Portuguese turfed up and blitzed the place like a bunch of bellends. Namely, De Sousa d'Arronches, and his band of merry yobos.

Today the town is of a modest size and carries with it an inoffensive bustle. I careered along one of its small sandy roads, merely a stone's throw from the coast. A whitewashed circular prism jutted up high above a lush crop of palms - it was the Dondra Head Lighthouse. And at 49 metres, it was the country's tallest of lighthouses. A British installation dating back to 1890, constructed from granite and steel and all sourced and shipped from the Britain Isles.

A short stretch inland, sits the modern day temple of Devundara Devalaya; a light blue coloured structure, representing the skin and aura of Lord Vishnu. I wondered what the enshrined God made of animal cruelty. For as I edged around the perimeter of the white walled compound a distressing sight struck me: a mother elephant chained to a tree. Several feet away, the mothers calf lay idle in a restrictive state of boredom. A hose pipe close by was rigged up to dribble water to lacklustre effect. The mothers eyes denoted sadness. Attached to a chain that couldn't have been any longer than 3 foot, she had no means of exercise, no means of playing with her daughter and certainly no means of freedom. She was a slave, plain and simple; and her calf was being robbed of its youth. As a whole, I'm largely respectful of others cultures and beliefs. I wouldn't have felt the need to visit such far flung places if I was anything but open minded in my approach to travel. Alas, this was a cruel and a sad sight to behold. It was no life for one of God's most beautiful of creatures.

Therefore, until certain trends change, I can only ever endorse a boycott of such a place. I felt useless and angry as I turned my back on mother and child, and continued west.

The coastal A2 towards Matara soon bulked up with traffic. Signboards bragged comfy rooms and tasty food, while posters pasted across ruined walls bore the beaming and no doubt fraudulent smile of a local politician. A boulevard of tightly parked cars faced the ocean as local families assembled to picnic and stroll along the shore front. At the far end of the boulevard a throng of buses and coaches loitered before the pedestrian footbridge to Pigeon Island; a small clump of rock and home to a quaint Buddhist garden temple. The city is situated at the mouth of the Nilwala River, adjacent a deep and well sheltered estuary. It became a valuable and strategic trading point for the Dutch, where they dealt largely in a trade of elephants and cinnamon. Fortified with two forts: the Matara Fort, that was said to be able to hold up to 80 elephants in its corral at any one time. And also the Star Fort, on the western bank of the river, built in the shape of a six-pointed star and poised to defend the surrounding area in all directions; but specifically from across the river - from where it was prone from attack. As was the case in what became known as the Matara Rebellion of 1761, when Sinhalese forces stormed the city and took the fort from the Dutch, albeit momentarily. For by 1762 , the Dutch had taken back control.

I weaved my way through the now gridlocked traffic as a flash with death soon came to pass me by. A gas cylinder, somehow dislodged, fell from the roof of a bus mere inches from my head - as it crashed onto the surface of the road and bounced off down the pavement in the direction of the beach. In truth, it was possibly one of the finest of gas cylinder escapades I had ever seen. And certainly, the best near death gas cylinder experience I'd ever had to date. Ideally, it would also be the last. I looked around slightly bewildered to see if anyone else had witnessed the aforementioned scenario. Nobody seemed to give a fuck. A man soon appeared atop the bus however, ostensibly satisfied with himself. I waved at him and pointed in the direction of the beach - 'he ran that way mate!' He waved back and told me that I was very cool. A comment about as useful as a fart in a colander, and all the same an interesting verse of rationale from someone that had nearly been responsible for the killing someone. I doubted very much that I looked cool though, bedraggled and sweaty, with trainers that hummed so bad that people could probably smell them from Jaffna. I was thankful in mind however that my number wasn't up just yet.

Slightly farther west along the coast, by a few short miles I wound up in the sleepy suburb of Polhena. I parked my bike up next to a dog with a massive set of bollocks and checked into the Tropi Turtle Guesthouse. A modest sized and airy beachfront property with a huge turtle mural on its compound wall. There were just a few other guests in my dorm: a mature Swedish couple that tried hard to read in peace over by the balcony as a shaggy haired, shirtless French lad with his dirty feet upon a small breakfast table obnoxiously FaceTimed.

I didn't dawdle long. And after I'd dumped down my possessions, I took a brief walk across the way to the ocean. Within moments of glancing across the shallow electric blue waters I caught sight of one of the seas most elegant of creatures. With gentle strokes of her flippers, she skirted around the darkened and cloddy patches of coral with the kind of articulate grace one might associate with an aquatic ballerina. She was undeniably a green turtle; the most common of Sri Lanka's five species of turtle. But for her to make it into adulthood would have been no easy feat. How she must've defied the odds is quite phenomenal, fighting the gauntlet from beach to ocean surrounded by her siblings in a mad dash for survival. With enemies at every turn: crabs, birds, dogs, fish, sharks, killer whales and of course that great destroyer: Man. It is no thanks to man, that the odds of a turtle even reaching adulthood are invariably slim. Through poaching and sea pollution such as plastic and oil spills, they also have to contend with miles upon miles of fishing nets - that alone are estimated to kill tens of thousands of individuals worldwide every year. It's said that just 5% of all newborn turtles across the globe reach adulthood. And then on top of all that, consider the fact that a green turtle doesn't reach sexual maturity on average until about 30 odd years of age. So in some respect, I was observing a miracle. She was magnificent. I watched her for sometime before eventually she gently slipped away into the coral and out of sight.

As night set in, I went in search for a cold brew, yet found nothing but disappointingly warm bottles of piss.

Polhena - Mirissa
6 miles

He rises early and moves towards the ocean. The light of dawn barely breaks the horizon. He treads the beaches soft sands that sink gently beneath his weight as he wades into the shallows; just like his father and that of his grandfather before him. There, amongst the coral, he scales a rickety looking pole to his vantage point upon a wooden crossbeam; known as a petta. Perched precariously, with a bag for catch by his side, he casts out his line. Then patiently, he waits.

On the road early, I caught a sight synonymous with many a travel guides and postcards that stem from the south coast of Sri Lanka: *Ritipanna* - aka, stilt fisherman. Their catch that is normally consistent of mackerel and herring, is very much dependant upon the season, and with an average earning of a mere 300 - 400 rupee a day, his life denotes one of poverty and hardship. To those that stop to take photos, film or even have a stab at stilt fishing themselves, a tip is a kindness always appreciated.

I follow the road which leads to Mirissa. I scarcely had to plan my route by this point. I merely perused the coast. The long and sweaty days in the saddle were now gradually drawing to a close. Instead, they were becoming short and sweaty. The tourist belt of the south coast tied the towns together with a mixture of booze, sun lotion, polyester and deck chairs. It was here in Sri Lanka that commercial tourism had truly staked its claim.

I found the Laid Back Gecko backpackers hostel and paid for a night in a 16-man dorm. The aroma within represented a mixture of stray farts and musky bed sheets. It was dark and dingy and I feared for what germs may have roamed. Instinctively, I clutched at my handlebar bag for some form of unbeknownst comfort. One of the hostel staff pointed out much to my annoyance, my designated top bunk. I despise top bunks, largely because that novelty wore off when I was about 8 years old. He then went on to inform me that there was also no water pressure and that the air con was busted. That helped to explain the abominable stench that still to this day lingers aghast and corrosive at the back of my mind. I went on to ask the member of staff when the water pressure might be back on, so that I might hopefully have a shower and perhaps wash away some sins. But, he had consequently slipped away into the shadows of the dorm. I'd never see him again. My only accompaniment now, bar the infernal stench, was a not so distant obnoxious snorefest from a few late night revellers powering through their respective hangovers. Getting some shut eye in such a place was going to be an issue. I huffed mildly and launched my gear onto my top bunk. There followed a mystery splattering noise. I exalted another huff before pissing off in the direction of the beach. In earnest, the only viable resolution to such a predicament.

The crescent shaped beach of Mirissa with its fringe of leaning palms, silky sands and calm, periwinkle blue waters, could almost be considered idyllic, almost. Problem being, when everyone gets that exact same memo, a place often becomes rife for overcrowding. There were scenes before me that were both terrible and immaculate. Yet largely the former. The sands were strewn with rows of tightly packed, sunbaked flesh. Skin so red raw in places that you could have peeled it right off the bone. A modest stroll along the beach often allows me to gauge population density ratios and whether or not I'm going to actually enjoy myself. I achieve this due to having an all round natural magnetism for all manner of flying objects: frisbees, footballs, rugby balls and occasionally beer bottles. The more that I come into contact with such paraphernalia, the more I don't feel the actual need to be at that specific locale in time. It's not even a question of well crafted avoidance, because believe me, I try really hard not to get hit by such flying tomfoolery. But largely, it is to no avail, something from somewhere will inevitably take me down. Generally, by the time I've actually found a spot in which to lay my towel, I'm normally so stressed out that I'd rather go and find a bar to get shit-faced in. On this occasion, I walked a mere 3 metres of beach before a frisbee hit me in my left titty. A pot-bellied slob in budgie smugglers with accompanying wafer thin model girlfriend (of whom I suspected of being Russians), laughed directly at my misfortune. Well then, that sealed the deal - my beach strolling days were over. I took a beeline directly to the nearest beach bar. If I was to gain any light satisfaction for the remainder of the day, then I was going to need at least six large bottles of ice cold beer, two refreshing mojitos and a nightcap of G & T. This would in effect, allow me to stagger home with perfection.

Mirissa - Unawatuna
18 miles

I awoke to a messy scene. My chest covered in a suspicious red substance. At first glance it appeared that I had been murdered. Yet, apart from a throbbing head that felt as if it had been run over by a rickshaw, there was little other pain to complain about, or any obvious wound for that matter. I wiped a finger across my chest and took a whiff of the red substance in question: tomato ketchup. This explained the ominous 'splat,' that I had heard upon check-in yesterday afternoon when I haphazardly tossed my belongings onto my top bunk and dispersed almost directly to the boozer. A little more investigating brought to my attention a popped open sachet of tomato ketchup. Some halfwits idea of a practical joke no doubt. A 'Ketchup Bandit' of little to no remorse, that quite clearly got off on the sheer tomatoey discomfort of others. I swore a little, and stumbled off my bunk. Grabbed my towel and headed for the shower.

It was a cursed place, a place that in the dead of night the mould within surely wept. Amongst a setup of stray bras and underpants, damp towels, a half eaten packet of chilli squid flavoured crisps, a bloodied sanitary pad sat next to a toothbrush and an absolute jungle of displaced pubic hair, I managed to locate the shower valve. I turned it. There was a gasp of air and a trickle of water so weak that even a 'Borrower' would have been offended. The water pressure was still fucked. I sighed, stole a crisp, and walked to the beach for an early morning dip.

The early bird gets the worm they say, or at least beats the tourist sun worshipping hoards. At a little after 6am, the sun had barley risen and I practically had the beach to myself. Albeit, a couple of beach puppies that tumbled playfully with one another in the sands. There was a comfort at being able to hear the waters loll against the shoreline in such a laid back agenda. Not a Russian trance song or a rogue frisbee in sight. I sunk into the cool relief of the ocean. An unrivalled and simple bliss. There I would remain until my head only felt like it had been shut in a car door a couple of times by Vinnie Jones. But, more important than that, I was no longer coated in a baselayer of tomato ketchup. For me, this was a most satisfactory outcome.

Back at the airless dorm, an historic fart cast by some greasy backpacker some 4 years previously, still gloated with guileless abandon. I chose not to loiter.

Naturally, someone had fiddled with my bicycle gears at some-point during the night. As no sooner had I began to pedal, than did my chain fall straight off. My fee for such, was the loss of a vast swathe of shin-skin. This however was nothing new. For often when the bike was sat idle and in the path of humans I found that they just couldn't seem to help themselves. It was just mostly harmless curiosity with a hint of annoyance that one just learns to live with. The fact that the bike was always where I had left it locked up for the night was the integral part.

The A2 coastal highway fed me through the popular surf destinations of Weligama, Midigama and Ahangama. Each village awash with surfers in their wetsuits either waxing up, or out in the waters hunting for breaks and swells. It is also along this section coast, along the Weligama bay, rising atop an islet, where there sits a lavish Neo-Palladian mansion. A place that until 1925, was a dumping ground for cobras. That was until the French born, eccentric British landscaper, garden designer and furniture maker Maurice Talvande, the self-styled Count de Mauny Talvande, purchased the rock for a mere 250 rupees. It was here that after ridding the rock of its collection of serpents, that he named the islet 'Taprobane,' after the Greek name for Sri Lanka. And there on in, sought to create his own private Eden and accompanying debonair lifestyle. The count is now long gone, but the islet is now considered a luxury getaway that has accommodated varying kings, queens, presidents, prime ministers and Kylie Minogue. I imagined that the islet didn't accept clammy wrecks on push bikes and that I could ill afford anything they may have had to offer on their breakfast menu. So I opted for avocado on sweaty bread at a local beach shack instead. On the table next to me, a young surfer with long blonde locks delicately opened a sachet of tomato ketchup, before applying it modestly to his scrambled eggs on sweaty bread. It appeared, that I had found my 'Ketchup Bandit.'

24. Galle
ගාල්ල දිස්ත්‍රික්කය
காலி மாவட்டம்

'The only way of discovering the limits of the possible is to venture a little way past them into the impossible.'
- Arthur C. Clarke

I cycle farther, knowing where it is that I am headed, but not where I am going. A contradiction of sorts that somehow just makes sense to me. My mind wanders wherever it wants. I think of my family, lost loves, squandered opportunities, drunken brawls, the darkness of the jungle at night, Tokyo and dying alone. With my journey so close to its climax, I found that the mind wandered and therefore wondered more than ever. Unlike in the early days of my venture, it was no longer entirely a no strings attached affair. Mixtures of merriment and darkness flowed through me like an unsteady tide. A series of women walking down the street that wore nothing but dental floss for bikinis soon distracted me. Along with tubby, topless men in weird white pants; often a bottle of alcohol in-hand and a cigarette pursed tightly between their lips. This evidently could only mean one thing - Russians. I'd clearly arrived in Unawatuna, a suburb or Galle, and one of the country's most famed of beach resorts. Along a narrow and winding street I cycled alongside a stretch of hip cafes and bars advertising happy hour, travel agencies with the best deals in the land, yoga retreats, guesthouses, eyesore hotels and shops selling more souvenirs, trinkets and handicrafts than you could possibly shake an emulsified boiled sausage at. English and Russian literature adorned these advertisements as the occasional rickshaw buzzed along noisily in an eager search for clientele. Intermittent breaks in this commercial sprawl allowed access to the beach; once deemed one of the top ten beaches in the world. However due to unregulated construction post the 2004 Boxing Day Tsunami devastation, many hotels and properties were built directly upon the beach that in some cases has created limited or restricted access. How different this must have all looked when Arthur C. Clarke first arrived here to live in 1956.

The Out of Rupeace hostel was a quiet and inoffensive hostel, tucked well away from the busy hum and thrum of the towns commercial hub. Even more importantly, it was spotlessly clean; not a pube in sight. Being the dorms only guest I was given free roam. Quite rightly, I picked a bottom bunk completely void of exploding tomato ketchup sachets. I laid back, weatherworn and slightly hung over, and had myself a little siesta.

I awoke revitalised and ready to tackle Rumassala; a forested rocky outcrop that rises up 58 metres to the north of Unawatuna Beach. Rumassala is the focal point of the area and stems from Sanskrit, meaning 'Rama's

Hall.' The etymology of Unawatuna also correlates to the said rock, translating roughly as / 'there, it fell.' In the epic Hindu story Ramayana, by the Indian poet Valmiki, it was written that Lakshmana, brother of Rama, got his shit fucked up whilst in battle with Ravana's demon army. In order to heal Lakshmana, the services of Hanuman, the incredulous leaping monkey God were sought. Hanuman was ordered to fetch some rare herbs that could only be found in the peaks of the Himalayas. So off he lept, straight across the Indian sub-continent and right up into the Himalayas. Just like that. But by the time Hanuman had made it up into the mountains he had forgotten what herb it was that he needed in order to cure Lakshmana. Not an issue for an all powerful warrior monkey God; for he just ripped out a solid chunk of Himalaya at the root and lept back to Sri Lanka with it under his arm. Some of the Himalayan rock crumbled on passage, where it fell across parts of both India and Sri Lanka. One such place this herbal-rich chunk of Himalaya was considered to have fallen was on the coasts of Galle - where I found myself stood at the base of my own not quite so epic tale. Today's surrounding forests that engulf the rock still boast an incredible richness of biodiversity that are believed to contain well over 150 medicinal herbs. Flora said to have cured Lakshmana, allowing him to continue his good fight against the demon hoards, and to dispatch of Ravana's two sons Indrajit and Atikaya; before some time later drowning himself in a river. For

Lakshmana, success was a bitch.

On foot, I took the road up the mini-mountain that was in places steep and narrow with the occasional death-defying rickshaw that required an element of assiduous dodging. A friendly jungle dog emerged from the undergrowth to say hello. I patted his head before he pottered up the hill ahead of me happily wagging his tail. For whatever sin he had just committed in the bushes, he was certainly most pleased with himself about it. After a steady ascent, a kinked and sandy path strayed away from the road. My new dog-friend and I journeyed down it in unison. The sides of the path were disappointingly strewn with litter; largely plastic. From somewhere up ahead music throbbed as the fragrant scent of spices cut through the humid air around us. Dog-friend's nostrils twitched and he upped his pace. As I stepped down from some black rocks and came to sea level an opening appeared from out of the jungle. A place where the waves dolefully trembled against the shore and the sands before them played host to the weekend crowd. Without turning back, Dog-friend barked about something unfamiliar to me before wading into a sea of burnt arses. He disappeared into the pell-mell of flesh, until all I could see was the excitable wagging of his tail that flitted back and forth like a hairy dorsal fin. Dog-friend had found his element.

Jungle Beach is a small sun-bed clustered cove that faces The Bay of Galle. As it was the weekend, the beach was a hive of activity, brimful of both local and western tourists alike. I sat upon the beach for a while and closed my eyes; as I listened to the panorama of sounds dotted about me: beer bottles clinked, a mixture of horrible music collided, something sizzled on on a frying pan, dog-friend barked, people laughed, sang and chatted in tongues unknown to me. I tried to channel them all out, so that it was nothing more than the gentle waters caressing the indulgent shore line. I soon began to drift away on the breeze like the lightest of feathers. A feeling of the utmost contentedness was somewhere close, it almost felt like something I could taste. I was having a moment. I delved deeper into the recesses of my mind. How could I take this humbling moment to the next level. THUD!! A frisbee hits me in the face and disrupts my moment of near nirvana. All the noises of the beach come flooding back to me in a banal surge of pure annoyance. A large man wearing very small and stereotypically weird white pants collects his frisbee without apologising. Russian. Regardless, my time here was up. Nirvana wasn't meant for me anyway.

I walked farther around the beach out onto some rocks that bordered the waters edge. There, I climbed back up and the crowds began to thin out somewhat. A mixture of equally distributed young local couples sat together either on the rocks or set back amongst the scrub. Some held hands and chatted as some sat in silence and listened to music on their mobile devices.

Others committed to fondling in the bushes ...literally. Yes, I'd found a sex people place.

I walked on swiftly, turning a blind eye to the varying acts that if I hadn't have had the internet since 1997, may well have warped my fragile little mind. Soon, at the edge of a precarious outcrop, I came to a halt. The water below me glinted as it lolloped up against the rocks. It was late afternoon by now and the views out across the bay towards Galle Harbour were hazy and uncertain; just as they may have been when the Portuguese first arrived some half a kiloyear ago. A moment that for Sri Lanka, would change her course of history for a very long time.

Unawatuna - Hikkaduwa
21 miles

In 1505, a stray fleet bound for the Maldives was swept off course, where it eventually found its way to a sheltered bay along the southern coast of Sri Lanka. The crowing of a cockerel was the first noise that the crew heard upon landfall, the Portuguese word for cockerel is '*galo*,' and therefore the modern day usage of Galle is said to have potentially stemmed from this. The town's roots however have been documented long before the arrival of the naval might of the Portuguese. For the Greek geographer Ptolemy, was said to have recorded the town in his 2nd Century world map, sometime between 125-150 AD. A bustling international trading port that saw the likes of the Romans, Persians, Malayans, Chinese, Indians, Arabs and Greeks all come to town to ply their trade. Some scholars have even suggested that Galle was the biblical land of Tarshish, a place far across the sea, from where King Solomon was thought to have acquired his wealth of gems, spices and exotic animals. Over the course of the 16th Century, the Portuguese succeeded in establishing trade with the Kingdom of Kotte. A trade partnership that ultimately led to a vice like colonial grip upon vast swathes of the island. Galle, being situated on a natural harbour, was of historic and strategic significance - upon which the Portuguese capitalised. And, by 1588, they had constructed an earthen fort with a rampart, three bastions and a northern wall of palisades. Here, they controlled the peninsula for some 62 years, until they were outmuscled and superseded and thus sent packing by the Dutch East India Company. With the Dutch at the helm, by 1663, they had completely renovated the fort across some 52 hectares, bolstering its fortifications with coral and granite, whereby they constructed an almost impenetrable rampart: 14 bastions, defended by 109 cannons, a grid layout of streets with buildings consistent of Tuscan columns and verandahs of 17th and 18th Century Dutch architecture. Today, it hones the status as a designated UNESCO World Heritage site and the largest remaining fortress in Asia constructed by colonial Europeans.

  I felt nimble as I slipped as delicately as I could

through the congested downtown traffic of Galle. I skirted the boundary of the international cricket stadium before coming to the heavyset rampart of Galle Fort. Tourists perused at a leisurely pace with expensive cameras draped around their necks. Its narrow brick work alleyways clustered with boutique cafes, Italian gelaterias, French creperies, fancy shops, fine dining restaurants, hip guesthouses, historic churches, chapels, mosques, temples, art galleries, clock towers, museums, a judiciary court, British school and a lighthouse that towers prominently over the harbour. The strikingly attractive and immaculately preserved streets and facades of the fort clearly reflected a passionate love for a place that Sri Lanka could now call her own.

I set my bicycle down next to the lighthouse and took a brisk walk along the ramparts. A row of trees shaded the path. A couple just wed were having their photographs taken. Their happiness rhapsodical and infectious to every passerby. I celebrate them by purchasing myself an ice cream. A simplistic and votive offering for them both - for me. The ice cream melts uncontrollably and I look like a fool. Yet, I don't really care.

Just 13 miles due north from Galle, past the watery expanses of the broad Gin River and Mahamodara and Rathgama Lakes, I came to Hikkaduwa. To the south of town and a short spell inland, I have to summit a steep set of steps evocative of the steps from 'The Exorcist,' in order to reach my guesthouse. I found myself having to conquer them twice over: once with my bicycle and again with my baggage. I melted just as efficiently as my ice cream some two hours previously.

In a stunning white villa with a well manicured lawn, I met my host, of whom was sat reading. His legs elegantly crossed in a well ironed white shirt and grey drainpipe trousers. A soppy looking doberman lay sprawled out by his heel; like nothing really mattered. The man looked up at me from the brim of his glasses as I bounded up onto the porch like an escaped tub of margarine. He committed himself to a dry smile. 'And you must be Daniel.'

'That I am,' I confirmed, as sweat poured out of me like a chronic masturbater.

'Welcome to Hikkaduwa Daniel, I've been expecting you. May I call you Danny?'

'Err..sure, why not?' - I'd certainly been called worse things in my time.

'Excellent,' he slammed his book shut with one hand and seemed satisfied as he rose to his feet, his doberman joining him in unison. 'I'm faus,' and held out his hand. 'And allow me to introduce you to Aragon.' Faus said something to the big black dog in Sinhala and the doberman gingerly stepped closer to me, I held out my hand to him and he sniffed it curiously, before deciding that it was worth a lick. I patted his head and it then appeared that Aragon was comfortable with my existence. 'You are now friends,' confirmed Faus, '-now allow me to show you to your living quarters.' Faus was well spoken and had an awe of pride in welcoming travellers to his hilltop retreat. For a retreat, I soon came to realise was essential for the recovery of the chaos that bred down on the sands of Hikkaduwa Beach.

*

The waves hacked away at the shoreline; strong and contentious. Surfers were out en masse, some of them mere dots on the horizon. Others, were being coached as they practiced their technique on dry land. Amongst the hawkers, the beach clientele were as varied as ever: the heavy breasted male beer guzzler, the sunbaked anus taking selfies, the sleepy reader with her book upon her face, the shameless couple that seem adamant to have their domestic in public, the phantom farter (guilty!), the screaming child, the depressed surfer picking shards of coral out of his broken foot, and those all important attention seeking doberman beach puppies. Aragon, that salty dog, had clearly been doing the rounds.

It was a long beach with no shortage of bars and restaurants. Like all manner of coastal towns along the south and south-west coast, Hikkaduwa had evolved beyond more than that of being just a quaint little fishing village. Its purpose now, to serve the influx of tourism that had skyrocketed to these shores post civil war. I walked through the crowds, doing well to dodge the reckless frisbees, footballs, drones and something that resembled that of a ninja star. When the crowds thinned I threw down my towel and ventured into the surf. I didn't get very far - as the first wave to come into contact with me had developed some sort of an ego problem. Whereby, it abrasively picked me up in its tumbling, overly-moist grasp, twisted me into a selection of weird knots, before ultimately slam-dunking me headfirst back upon the beach into a of pile crumpled flesh and gristle. Something in my neck cracked horribly upon impact with the sand that appeared at the time to have the consistency of concrete. Instinct saw me crawl back pathetically to my towel, where for some hour or so I lay as still as possible in the utmost pain. I drifted off.

*

Fuck the sea, the sea is an arsehole, I declared as I drowned another beer. Potentially my 6th, or was it my 7th? When I came too, it was apparent that I'd pulled a muscle of some description in my neck (or just severed a nerve!). The cure for me was clearcut though, drink the pain away. Not that I needed many excuses to drink, but in this instant, it was obvious.

As night edged in, the beach bars lit up and the music seemed to pump louder and more hideously by the hour. Characters of a dubious nature congregated. Many travellers seemed to know the bar staff, locally referred to as beach boys as they grasped hands like old friends or accomplices. The same beach boys that constantly offered me drugs every time I went over for a beer.

'Dan ya fat twat!' Blurted a voice from amongst the din as a young man-bunned traveller approached and put a brotherly arm around me. An elasticated smile stretched the broadness of his face, it revealed a broken front tooth, like he'd chipped it trying to eat precious metals whilst off his tits on beach smack. I awkwardly had no memories of this person that was so implicitly comfortable with labelling me a 'fat twat.'

'Err...alright mate?' I don't think I was quite drunk another to speak to a stranger that I might know. I hadn't even had a mojito yet.

'Fucked any Russians yet?' His face was flushed and dripped sweat as his eyes darted in their respective sockets like a high-tempo game of Pong. It made no difference to what my answer may have been as there was scarcely room to get a word in edgeways. He rattled on about everything and nothing as I in turn zoned out from the drivel. A short way across the bar to the furore of an all encompassing 'WEYYYYY!!!!' - Some beach boys had encouraged a young American girl to flash her breasts in exchange for a shot. Thankfully, this vulgar act of exploitation and degradation had distracted man-bun features enough, that I could take my cue to slip away and migrate to some place more placid farther down the beach. It was time for my mojito. After which, I would no longer be at the handlebars.

***
Hikkaduwa - Bentota
23 miles

I started late. Hungover. Fucked really. Faus had to give me a knock on the door to make sure I still alive. Aragon stayed away, he could smell my drunken transgressions no doubt. The sun, relentless in its pursuit, beat down upon me like it had never done so before. At least, it felt that way. To nearly break ones neck and then to get shitfaced and jump on a bicycle in 32°c of heat wasn't big, and it certainly wasn't clever. But it was essential for my detox, I'd drunk a lot over the past week. Almost as if I was trying to catch up with all the booze that I'd failed to administer between the ages of zero to fourteen. The consequence now was that my body felt like it had spent a week in a tumble dryer. And so, there and then I declared my mojito binge to be over (until the next time).

The cycling to begin with was a misery. Amplified some 3 miles north of downtown Hikkaduwa to my arrival at the village of Peraliya. A huge beige Barmiyan Buddha replica statue, known as the Tsunami Honganji Vihara, stands some 18.5 metres tall upon a manmade island in the middle of a pond. His hand raised in the *Abhayamudrā*, a gesture of fearlessness. The Buddha is the exact same height as the second wave that tore through this very village on December 26th, 2004. Of the 430 homes in the area, only 10 remained after the tsunami. 500 villagers lost their lives and 200 more were swept out to sea, never to be found. 99.8% of Periliya was destroyed. At the exact time that disaster struck, the regular Queen of the Sea passenger train was travelling from Colombo to Galle. The first wave brought the 8 carriage train to a halt, creating an initial panic and pandemonium. The second and much larger wave, proved to be far more ruthless and deadly. The train and its carriages being derailed, and like the information board by the Buddha statue reads: 'tossed around like match boxes.' Over 1,700 passengers would perish, many drowning in the crowded carriages where they were unable to escape their ultimate fate.

A small and very graphic museum to the side of the pond depicted the stark realities of that fateful day. Somewhere in the area, one of the ruined carriages was also on display. But my dark touristic curiosity had already peaked; to linger longer just felt sadistic. The pain and misery caused along these shores shall reverberate and carry across this paradisiacal island for many years to come. I left Perilya deflated and equally as queasy as I'd arrived. Somehow, I already fancied a pint.

At the halfway point, between Hikkaduwa and Bentota, I pulled up under the shade of a cluster of palms to take a break from dying of perspiration. I hadn't stopped long before a man on a moped pulled up alongside me. His face was unquestionably a daunting one; one to proverbially scare the toothpaste back into its tube. And for a man on a motorised vehicle he was sweating quite intensely, almost as much as an alcoholic on a pushbike. He looked me up and down. 'What is...problem?' He asked, his words slurred. He'd clearly been on the toddy.

'Erm...no problem feller, just taking five, thanks,' I confirmed. He didn't seem very satisfied with my answer, as he continued to oogle me up and down with his dark, bloodshot eyes like some sort of desirable meat. He was certainly beginning to make me feel rather uncomfortable. 'You err....alright?' I enquired. He then looked me dead in the eyes and made everything abundantly clear to me.

'Sex?' The cat was out of the bag. It appeared that he was after a cheeky bum in the jungle - or a jungle bum if you please.

'Ooohhhh...I see!' Suddenly a little taken back and not so overly flattered. 'I think I'll be alright thanks.' He narrowed his eyes in a somewhat irascible demeanour before he wobbled off his moped and lumbered aggressively towards me. With clenched fists he shouted waspishly a mean sounding set of indecipherables. 'Oh for fucks sake, that was definitely a 'No' by the way,' I confirmed. Was he really just planning on taking what he wanted? Well, not on my fucking watch. I grabbed my heavy duty motorbike chain from the back of my bicycle rig and shook it out so that it unravelled and clinked to dramatic effect down by my side. 'You best be on your way-' I paused slightly, something was missing '-chap!' Just like the cockney geezer that I clearly wasn't and didn't ever really aspire to be. And yes, not the best of one liners, I fully admit that. Very crap in fact. Especially when you factor in such silver screen beauts like "go ahead, make my day," "you're gonna eat lightening and you're gonna crap thunder," or quite simply "bring it, you slag!" But in reality, when someone is showing signs that they plan to forcibly sodomise you in a jungle miles from anywhere you have to kind of think and act on your feet. Thankfully upon on seeing my big "fuck off"chain, the horned up aggressor stopped in his tracks. I then pointed to the road ahead and in no uncertain terms gestured for him to clear off. He muttered something and showed me the venom in his eyes. He really wasn't a very pleasant bloke, but he'd clearly got the message and was at least on his way. I hoped that was the last I would see of him and that he didn't have any counterpart sexual deviants up ahead waiting in limbo. For if there was one thing apart from alcohol that I'd clearly had enough off by this point, it was nutty fuckers on mopeds in the middle of the jungle.

By that stage, and probably quite rightly so, I had fully sobered up as I continued to cycle on the rest of the way to Bentota; my nerves slightly jangled. The remainder of the journey however was every bit as uneventful as I'd have hoped.

Bentota, being only 60 odd miles south from capital Colombo, is the ideal getaway for Colombites and short stay tourists. A resort town that is largely consistent of high end all inclusive hotels and fancy pants restaurants. Such as personal tradition though, I'd managed to find myself an inland retreat that had an all round aroma of stale piss. With its bathroom that looked like a crime scene and a bedroom that appeared to have somehow contracted jaundice. I had however, stayed in worse, a lot worse.

It was late afternoon as I took one final stroll along the shores of Sri Lanka. Along a sparsely populated stretch that seemed to trail away for as far as the eye could see. A far throw from the packed party crowds further to the south. I walked in my solitude and contemplated a mixture of everything and nothing; what I had seen and what I had done. A daydream within a daydream. Immaterial thoughts largely a buildup of irreplaceable memories that will only ever really be relevant to ones self. But I'll write about some of them anyway, I figured. Perhaps someday, someone, somewhere, might just find them interesting.

By a rocky outcrop some metres offshore, amongst the emerald blue waters of the Laccadive Sea, a common tern hunted for a meal. It floated delicately above the waves like a handkerchief caught in the wind, before it dived torpedo like into the surf. A hardened traveller and master of its trade. This little bird is well known for travelling well in excess of 35,000 km annually to and from its breeding grounds across much of Europe, North America and Asia. An aspiring feat to be marvelled at by any standards. One that clearly mocked my own travel exploits.

As I wandered back to my guesthouse to roost, I wondered if this journey would be my last long distance migration. I then envisioned the alternative: a cold and miserable trudge along the windswept eastern shores of England; amongst the fag butts, dog shit and anti-social behaviour. Well, it didn't take much for me to make my mind up on that one. Migration was clearly as much in my genetic makeup now as it was a flighty terns. Therefore, until my mortal ticket gets punched, I had no doubts that I'd be back on the road again sometime. This thirst for travel, it's contagious.

That night, I dreamt that I was far, far away. Farther than I'd ever need to be and farther than I was ever going to be. But I was there all the same, and somehow that was exactly where I needed to be.

25. Kalutara
කළුතර දිස්ත්‍රික්කය
களுத்துறை மாவட்டம்

*'The man who fell into the pit at night,
does not fall into it again in broad daylight.'*
- Sinhalese proverb

Bentota - Colombo
40 miles

Dread crept into my sleep around about the time dawn broke. A sound that haunted and chilled to the bone as the surrounding silence was breached. A sound that even if you had never heard it in your life would have you on your feet as a matter of urgency. It was a sound that I recognised chiefly as an air-raid siren, others perhaps the civil defence system; one I'd only ever heard in educational material at school and from old war films. Generally, a sound that without question that was associated with an imminent danger. In this case, being so close to the coast it could only realistically mean one thing: a tsunami.

To say it was squeaky bum time would have been an understatement. I ran to the window to check for commotion. It was still dim outside, but it mattered not as a line of palms obscured my view of the ocean. I looked over at the neighbouring property for movement

- a sign of fear, panic, screams and people running for the hills. Yet, I saw none of this. All was still. I was on the second floor of the guesthouse, *am I high enough?* I thought. I guess you'll soon find out! I countered, not filling myself with much confidence. I hastened out of my room and into the halls of the guesthouse. The siren echoed and amplified as I passed through into a sticky looking lounge area. Empty. Not a soul. Was I the last of my kind? And before things were allowed to get too deep the siren suddenly cut out. I emerged from the living room and out onto a balcony. The silence of dawn had regained its dominance as light slowly grew. I stood and waited, still unsure about how to proceed. A dry scraping noise soon started up from somewhere to the west of the property. I followed the balcony around until I saw an old man in his garden, sweeping up fallen leaves with a stiff broom. He seemed far from alarmed. Clearly, the warning systems were just getting a casual early morning test-run for any impending and needless to say catastrophic event. Probably a standard around these parts, probably. Well, panic over I figured, and took the old man's carefree nature to be my cue to return to my sleeping duties. And, as I lay back down in sheets covered in various forms of historic sin, an abrupt thought came to me, *what if the old man's deaf?*

    I was soon back in the saddle. Racing along through Kalutara; an area famed for its mangosteen production and the Kalutara Chaitya: a hollow three storey Buddhist stupa with an interior of 74 murals depicting the life of Buddha. A collection of shops, petrol stations, banks and ramshackle fruit and vegetables stalls aligned the rapidly evolving A2 as I drew ever closer to my return to Colombo. And before long, a dusty, polluted and overcrowded street became a three laned highway of infinite mayhem. Alas, with little alternative, this was just the way. I cycled on, back into the belly of the urban beast, from whence I came.

Colombo : A Return
කොළඹ දිස්ත්‍රික්කය
கொழும்பு மாவட்டம்

'Die with memories, not dreams.' - Unknown

An eternal commotion ensued, the endless ambient rumpus of this fast paced city could only ever intensify. The inner-city climes an explicit grade of gammy as traffic spreads through its nonsensical streets (and pavements) like mechanical bindweed. The buses become less forgiving, edging millimetres from flesh and bone; as opposed to just mere centimetres. People crushed together along the sidewalks become fair game as motorbikes thrash amongst them. Still, children find space for a game of cricket on a raised central reservation. Nearby, an elderly man sits upon a fold up chair to read the headlines in his newspaper. Everything was seemingly as I had left it. Nothing ever seemed steady in Colombo, if it did, it would surely be out of place.

My return to the hostel that I had departed some two months previously was unceremonious. Stuffy and airless, the fetid smell of the dorm greeting me like an old friend. I picked a bunk with bloodstained sheets (the only bunk available) and staked my claim by launching my dirty duffle bag upon it. I was starved and was set to go straight out for a bite to eat, but decided to curiously follow the staircase in the opposite direction to the streets - and thus ascend the gloomy flight of concrete steps to the buildings summit. Rats scarpered in the stairwells and from behind closed doors I could hear the muffled sounds of blaring television sets. By the time I'd reached the top I was as saturated in sweat, just as I were the day I'd first come to Sri Lanka, and every day since.

The final door that led to the buildings rooftop had been jarred open with a crowbar. It acted as a cool funnel of wind that soothed my soggy body. From atop the six-storey building, Colombo could be seen in a new light, almost as a new world: The Rooftop World. From the south, a series of morbidly dark clouds beckoned as a storm approached; it looked dramatic in every sense. The din of traffic still wallowed and anonymously honked from somewhere down below. At eye level there was a mishmash of suburban architecture: colonial, modern, Asian and homebrew. Buildings with exposed and crumbling brickwork and corrugated rooftops that sat humbly alongside 100 metre high shards of glass.

A crow joined me, perching itself on a railing some 3 feet away. It tilted its head to weigh me up and down. Content, it began to preen itself.

On the neighbouring building, from a precariously bendy TV aerial, a pair of bulbuls perched tightly together. Close by, a cornflower blue water tank leaked water across its mottled white rooftop floor, where in the middle of the puddle a broken sun-bed lay collapsed in a heap. From the next building over, a topless pigeon fancier appeared from a rickety old coop, a pigeon in hand. He stroked the bird delicately as he walked to the periphery of the rooftop. I noticed a huge scar that ran the length of his face; from temple to lower cheek. A scar from a previous life I imagined; either that, or an extremely bad tempered pigeon. We caught one another's eyes and he smiled gaily and waggled his head. One of the many beautiful smiles and head waggles that I'd encountered across this jewel of an island; everyone of them etched into my hippocampus like an internal cicatrice of worthy repute. Holding his bird in one hand he pointed to the skies that grew ever darker. I acknowledged his warning and waggled my head to reciprocate. My reply meant everything and nothing, or anything I wanted it to mean. That much I now knew. The man laughed.

I'd miss this contrasting country upon departure. From the sunbaked roads that led me into the island's rugged interior, through to its tea plantations and mythical mountain peaks, down their slopes and into its once war ravaged jungles that are burdened so deep with scars that time will never heal them. I'd pass through open plains where wild elephants grazed and along stretches of coast so ethereal at times it barely felt real. Roads that traversed a fusion of settlements - sleepy and chaotic and sometimes quite simply terrifying. For long periods of my lonesome sundrenched days in the saddle, where the heat more often than not tore my mind apart, these roads and accompanying particulars felt like this adventure truly was my own to be had. And, it was. To tackle the personal unknown, a land so alien to one's own and to reap the rewards of everything new there is to learn about a culture, a people and its history. For me, this is enlightenment. The road and everything I learnt from it, was my religion.

Droplets of rain metamorphosed into something more malevolent as I considered whether or not after the venturing of the previous months, if I felt a certain amelioration of self? Well, honestly? No, not really. There was an inveterate passion for the road, that much was certain. A passion that l will struggle to shake when and if the time should ever come to deflate my tires so to speak. What I felt personally though, that acted as the port of most significance, was the feeling that I didn't want to waste a moment in time when I had managed to create a vacuum for it. An opportunity had arisen to make the most of a moment, something that I felt as I matured would become increasingly less likely. Like dust, we all settle.

The irritable skies rolled ever closer. Children's voices amplified from the streets below as a train rumbled past. A dog barked and the brightly coloured bulbuls dispersed, leaving the TV antenna swinging dangerously free. Treetops shook and palmyra rustled, there was a solid thud as a coconut crashed to earth. A page from a newspaper took to the skies and whipped across the Colombo skyline and into a rapidly descending darkness. From behind a forested rooftop of potted plants that sat in blossom, a woman manically collected her laundry as she muttered curses in Sinhala.

    I looked back over towards the pigeon fancier, but he was gone.

    The crow cawed at me and departed for the coast.

    Out there, there were many more lands to explore. I'd never see them all and that was just the way it would have to be.

    The rain began to hammer down in excess and I decided to stay put. For a while, I lived for the moment. I must do it again sometime.

THE END

www.ingramcontent.com/pod-product-compliance
Lightning Source LLC
Chambersburg PA
CBHW030432010526
44118CB00011B/608